The United Methodist Member's Handbook

George E. Koehler

DISCIPLESHIP RESOURCES

PO BOX 340003 • NASHVILLE, TN 37203-0003
www.discipleshipresources.org

DEDICATION

This book is presented to:

_____

as a gift from our congregation:

_____

So then you are no longer strangers and aliens, but you are citizens
with the saints and also members of the household of God.
Ephesians 2:19

Fourth printing: 2008

ISBN 978-0-88177-219-7
Library of Congress Catalog Card No. 97-66504

Quotations from the *Discipline* are from *The Book of Discipline of The United Methodist Church—2004.* Copyright © 2004 The United Methodist Publishing House. Used by permission.

Quotations from the *Hymnal* are from *The United Methodist Hymnal.* Copyright © 1989 The United Methodist Publishing House. Used by permission.

Scripture quotations, unless otherwise indicated, are from the New Revised Standard Version of the Bible, copyright © 1989 by the Division of Christian Education of the National Council of the Churches of Christ in the USA. All rights reserved. Used by permission.

DR219

Contents

An Invitation

*P*lease consider this book a personal invitation to you from our congregation. We want you to find the sort of relationship in our church that is fulfilling for you, for us, and for Christ's mission in this place.

What's the nature of your church membership right now? You may be "just looking" and exploring the possibility of membership with us. You may have already decided on membership here but want an overview before taking your vows. You may have "been around here for years" but want to review what membership is all about. Whether or not you are now a member, whether you are a youth or an adult, whether or not you have ever been baptized or made a faith commitment, we believe this handbook will help you take important next steps.

What steps? We've discovered that faithful participation in the church involves three kinds of activity, and it is around these themes that this handbook is organized:

- To be a full member is to **belong.** Just "joining" or "attending" a church is not membership. We invite you to become an active, living part of this fellowship, one who belongs in the deepest sense.

- To be a full member is to **remember.** We live within the long stream of Judaic-Christian tradition. We want you to join us in celebrating and loving this story, and to find your place within it.

- To be a full member is to **believe.** We're a people who put our trust in God as revealed in Jesus Christ. We have not "arrived," but we're growing in faith and in doctrine, and we want to help you do this too.

Come join us in this adventure of belonging, remembering, and believing!

Whether you're using this handbook as an individual or as part of a group, we suggest you not only read it but also probe the questions and suggestions at the end of each topic. For further study, use some of the resources listed on page 94. And if you're a leader of a study group, please see the suggestions on pages 95-96.

May the Holy Spirit be your guide as you consider your membership in The United Methodist Church.

Part One

We Belong

Are you a hand? An ear? A foot? In his letters, the apostle Paul wrote that the church is like a human body. As members of the church we are likened to the different parts of the body. "Now you are the body of Christ and individually members of it" (1 Corinthians 12:27). But more than that: "He is the head of the body, the church" (Colossians 1:18).

Yes, to be a member of the church is to be a part of Christ's body, a functioning member of the whole, directed by Christ himself. What an astonishing image! What does this mean for our membership?

It means that the church is alive. It's not a building, a program, or a list of names. The church is a living organism. It's an integrated whole, like the human body. It has virtues, but it also has faults. It may be wounded, and it may also be healed. It has dreams and works toward making these dreams come true, but it often falls short. The church is ever changing, growing, and moving.

To be the body of Christ means that members of the church are different from one another. As Paul pointed out, not all are feet or hands, ears or eyes. We differ according to our various gifts. We differ in age, sex, race, abilities, temperament, even in our beliefs. Yet we are one. (See Romans 12:4-5.)

All members are needed. "If the foot would say, 'Because I am not a hand, I do not belong to the body,' that would not make it any less a part of the body" (1 Corinthians 12:15).

The head of the Body is Christ. It is our living Lord who gives purpose and direction to the church. Without such direction, the Body would flounder helplessly. But if the various members attend to the will of Christ together, they can move forward as a coordinated whole.

What is your place in the body of Christ? Do you feel that you truly belong to the whole? What particular gifts do you bring that contribute to the Body's purpose? What steps can you take to become a more fully functioning part of the church? These are questions you will want to ask yourself as we explore, in Part One, the meaning of belonging to a United Methodist congregation.

1 We Belong to a Congregation

How do we become members of the body of Christ? It happens through belonging to a particular congregation of God's people. Not just joining, but truly belonging. It's in that fellowship that we come to see ourselves as part of Christ's body and part of God's family.

Belonging is a two-way street, isn't it? In part, it's a gift. We cannot earn it. We cannot force it. The sense of belonging comes when we have spent some time in a fellowship of caring people, joined with them in some meaningful activities, perhaps struggled with some difficult issues, and upheld one another in love.

Though a gift, belonging is also something we do. We need to be actively present. We need to extend ourselves to others, sometimes taking the initiative in conversation and in care. We need to be open, ready for new relationships, new insights, and new responsibilities. When we put our whole selves into active participation with other Christians, the gift of belonging will gradually find us. This process takes place at several levels, in what we might call "circles of belonging."

Relationships with other people

At the most direct and personal level, we belong to other people. We see, as Ephesians puts it, that we're "members of one another" (4:25). I'm a member of you, and you're a member of me. We speak our hearts to each other, listen to each other, care for each other.

This does not happen, of course, if we only sit in the pew. It does not even happen through taking part in all kinds of groups and programs if we do not make ourselves available to others. To belong to other people we will need to make time for them in our lives, to stop and pay attention to them, to respond. It may mean visiting over coffee at the kitchen table, listening with concern at a hospital bedside, extending a hand at school or on the job. We can help one another belong.

Small groups

The gift of belonging is also received as we take part in the small groups of the congregation. In a church school class, a fellowship or service group, or a group for planning and leading the work of the church, we find our own special place. We meet people, share concerns, serve in a common mission. The small group offers a church in miniature, where we can come to belong more easily. We all need these small groups.

The congregation as a whole

Little by little, as we come to know more people, as we participate regularly in the congregation's life and take on responsibility for its work, we discover that we truly belong at that level too. We stop saying "that church" or "their church" and start saying "our church." Its mission is our mission.

The United Methodist Church

As we take our membership vows in the congregation, we become full members of our denomination as well. We deepen our sense of belonging in The United Methodist Church as we become more familiar with its forms of worship, its hymnal, and its church school curriculum resources. And we broaden our membership as we get acquainted with Methodists from other congregations through the work of our church at district, annual conference, national, and international levels.

The whole church

Through baptism and profession of faith (see topics 29 and 30), we're initiated not only into this congregation but also into the worldwide church of Jesus Christ, made up of all peoples, nations, and denominations. Our sense of belonging to the ecumenical church is deepened as we take part with other Christians in the whole work Christ is asking us to do.

Christ invites you to belong to his church and to deepen your sense of participation and fellowship in all these "circles of belonging." In the remaining pages of this first section, we explore many of the ways you may do this.

For Reflection

1. What can you do in the months ahead to belong more fully to your congregation?
2. What opportunities for small groups does your congregation offer?

United Methodist

2 We Have a Mission

Why does the church exist? According to Matthew's Gospel, the risen Christ made it clear: "Go therefore and make disciples of all nations, baptizing them in the name of the Father and of the Son and of the Holy Spirit, and teaching them to obey everything that I have commanded you" (28:19-20).

Based on this "Great Commission," our United Methodist Church has stated its purpose: "The mission of the Church is to make disciples of Jesus Christ. Local churches provide the most significant arena through which disciple-making occurs" (From *The Book of Discipline of The United Methodist Church—2004,* p. 87. Copyright © 2000 by The United Methodist Publishing House. Used by permission).

So the mission of our congregation is to make disciples. This is a four-fold task.

We reach out to people and welcome them into the church

We have a direct responsibility for people of the "world" around our church, the community in which we and others study, work, shop, play, and so forth. In this world are people with many hurts, doubts, and questions. There are some who are new in the community and feel a little lost, some who are proudly self-sufficient, and others who are in desperate circumstances. Our mission is to reach out to them, listen to them, accept them, share the gospel in word and deed, invite them into the family of faith, and joyfully receive all who will respond.

We relate people to God and help them deepen their relationship with God

The second task in making disciples is to offer people opportunities for growing closer to God. Whether they are visitors or old-time members, just beginning the journey of faith or well along the road—all are in need of God's love in Christ. Through worship, prayer, study, and honest sharing, we help one another discover that the Holy Spirit is not far off but present with us, wanting an open and loving friendship with each of us—not only friendship but commitment as well. Through our congregation's various ministries we encourage one another to give our selves to Christ, to ground our lives in the living God.

We nurture people in Christian living

Third, our congregation's mission is to nurture people of all ages in the Christian faith and to help them practice the disciplines of discipleship. The church exists not to serve itself but to serve the world. We come to church not only for our own personal enrichment but also to prepare our-selves to do the work of love and to get ready to be Christ's disciples in the community. Through worship, baptism, Communion, Bible study, prayer, and other means of grace, we're strengthened for ministry.

We support people in their ministry

As members of the congregation, we're sent into the community to serve those in need and to make our community more loving and just. We believe that the Holy Spirit empowers and guides us in these ministries and that wherever there's need and suffering, we meet Christ, already at work. But still, we cannot be effective in ministry on our own. So the con-gregation exists, in part, to surround and support each member in his or her ministry. We do not always succeed in our efforts to be faithful disci-ples in the world. But with the loving support of the community of faith, we can continue to grow.

We could abbreviate our mission as one of *welcoming-worshiping-nurturing-sending.* (See *The Book of Discipline of The United Methodist Church—2004,* p. 88, and *Guidelines for Leading Your Congregation: 2005-2008.*) In the next five topics of this handbook, we'll explore specific ways in which our congregation works at this fourfold mission.

For Reflection

1. With your pastor or other leader, complete the worksheet, "Our Congregation at a Glance," on page 92.
2. How does your congregation's understanding of its mission compare with the church's mission discussed above?

Member's Handbook

3 We Witness

To belong to our congregation is to share the gospel with others. It's to tell in word and deed the good news of God's love for all people as revealed in Jesus Christ.

Gospel is the English translation of the New Testament word for good news, which we sometimes abbreviate as *evangel.* So we call our sharing of the "good news" with those who are not yet Christians, evangelism. Or we say that we "witness" to the gospel, meaning that we convey to others what God's good news has meant in our lives. Such witnessing may involve these five related ministries:

Reaching

First, we reach out to people. We greet them and speak with them. We let them know that we're interested in them and in their lives. We listen to what they have to say and express our concern. We do this with friends and relatives, with schoolmates, co-workers, and neighbors—both those well known to us and strangers. Along with others of the congregation, we may call on people in their homes.

Sharing

Second, we share the gospel. Where appropriate, we talk about our own journey of faith, the ups and the downs, and how we're currently growing. We ask others about their journeys. We point to Jesus as the source of our strength and salvation. We may tell a little of the biblical story of salvation. No, we do not pretend to have all the answers. Rather, in the spirit of concerned friendship, we simply speak of what we have known of God's love.

Inviting

Third, we invite people to take part in this congregation. We have discovered something here worth sharing with others—a special kind of caring fellowship, a sense of God's presence in worship, a new understanding of the Bible, and a way to join with others in making a difference in the world. We tell others about the congregation and urge them to visit.

Bringing

Fourth, we bring others with us to church. We know that often just inviting others to come will not be enough. It's more friendly and more effective to ask, "When can we pick you up?" We may bring them to the Sunday morning worship service as our guests or to our church school class. We may invite them to a group outing, such as the softball team's practice, to a special music or drama event at the church, or to a Christmas Eve service. And then we bring them again. We take the opportunity to introduce them to others, including our pastor. Once they have tasted our congregation's fellowship a few times, it will be up to them to decide about returning.

Asking

Finally, at appropriate times we ask people the question of faith: "Are you ready to ground your life in God as revealed in Jesus Christ?" Or, "Will you answer Jesus' call to follow him?" Or, "Will you receive God's love and live by faith?" The words we use will vary. We put God's question before other people; we raise with them the issue of their response to the good news. We're not responsible for the answers others give. We're responsible for asking the question.

We witness in these five ways not only through what we say but also by how we act. Words without actions are empty; actions without words leave no clue as to their source, the gospel. Both words and deeds are needed. Will you be such a witness for Christ?

For Reflection

1. List opportunities you have for witnessing. Share candidly the factors that make it difficult to witness. How can people in your church support one another in the task of witnessing?
2. Review your congregation's plans for evangelism. Share ideas for improving the church's witness. The experience of new members or inquirers can be most valuable.

United Methodist

4 We Worship

To belong to our congregation is to join regularly in the worship of God. Worship is probably the most distinctive thing we do as Christians. The service of corporate worship is the central event of our congregation's life. But exactly what is worship?

Meeting God

Worship is an opportunity to meet God. We come into worship full of expectation that through the Spirit, God will be present, we will speak to God, and God will speak to us.

We praise the Lord, our Creator and Sustainer. In ritual and song and prayer, we address God. But we also take time to listen—to receive God's forgiving love, to respond to the quiet stirrings of the Spirit in our hearts. Worship is a two-way communion with the living God.

Celebrating our faith

Worship is also a time of celebration. In a way it's like a birthday party or a parade. We remember the wonderful things God has done and rejoice. We give thanks for God's many gifts, especially for the gift of Jesus Christ, alive now in our midst. We dedicate ourselves anew to lives of Christian discipleship, to ministry with one another and in the world.

Our celebrations are organized around an annual calendar of remembered events, the "church year." We relive crucial episodes of God's revelation in Christ in a cycle of six seasons: Advent, Christmas, Sundays after Epiphany, Lent, Easter, and Sundays after Pentecost. Through Scripture, drama, music, colors, and other means, we take part in the ancient story.

We take part especially through singing. We United Methodists love to sing the songs of faith. Our *Hymnal* is a collection of hymns for all seasons in a variety of styles—traditional, gospel, spiritual, and ethnic. In the spirit of our Methodist founder, John Wesley, we make "a joyful noise to the LORD" (Psalm 98:4).

Relating God's Word to our lives

Worship is a way of making connections between the Bible and our lives. The Bible is our book, the story of our origins, the written account of God's relationship with humankind. As we read the Bible with curiosity and openness, we find that the Holy Spirit speaks to us.

As we hear the Bible in worship, through prayer, and through the sermon, the biblical message is brought into contact with the issues of everyday life. Worship is not a time to "put on our best face" and leave behind our personal concerns. It's a time to bring these concerns and those of the world before God, and to listen for the Scriptures' direction.

Taking part in the sacraments

At the center of worship is the sacrament of Holy Communion, or the Lord's Supper. And at the beginning of our Christian life is the sacrament of baptism. We will examine these sacraments more closely later. (See topics 29 and 36.)

Growing in our devotional life

In addition to our worship as a congregation, we worship individually and as families. Many people in our congregation find that the daily disciplines of Bible reading and prayer are essential for their continuing fellowship with God. Many use a small devotional guide, such as *The Upper Room, Alive Now,* or *Weavings.* These are available from The Upper Room (See "For Further Study," p. 94.)

For Reflection

1. For a deeper understanding of your congregation's worship services, study a copy of the order of worship with your pastor.
2. Discuss various devotional patterns with others. Look over a number of devotional guides and discuss their use. If you do not have a regular devotional practice, commit yourself to a plan for two weeks, and then evaluate it.

Member's Handbook

5 We Learn

To belong to our congregation is to be a learner, seeking to grow in faith and discipleship. But *how* do we learn the Christian faith? How do we learn to be disciples of Christ?

We learn in countless ways: from our families, from Christian friends, in services of worship, from drama and film, and by just living and working together in the congregation. But we also learn by being taught, by studying together in church school classes and other groups—that is, through Christian education.

In our church the goal of Christian education is the development of Christian faith and discipleship. Christian education is not just learning about the Bible or the church. It is not just understanding and accepting certain Christian beliefs. These are important paths in our growth, but the central purpose of Christian education is growing in faith and discipleship. This growth happens as we respond to God's guiding through at least four influences.

The Bible

We're a people of the Book. We find in it a long and varied story of God's relationship with humankind. And for us this story is the foundation of faith and discipleship. It's the source of our beliefs, our values, our moral decisions, and our actions.

In our Christian learning we approach the Bible in two ways. We may start with the Scriptures—a story, a teaching, a character, a whole book of the Bible. We read the words. We explore the text, trying to understand what it meant to its first hearers and readers. Then we look for implications for our own lives, our community, and our world.

Or we may begin with modern life, with a personal or social issue, and then go to the relevant sections of the Bible for insight and a deeper understanding of God's will for the situation. In either case we build a bridge between God's Word and current life.

The teacher

Thank God for teachers! Many of us can testify to the important influence of church school teachers, youth counselors, or other education leaders in our lives. The teacher is a guide, interpreting the Bible and the other riches of our tradition. The teacher is a coach, a planner, and a director of learning activities. Best of all, the teacher is a person, a counselor and friend, and often a model as well.

The class

We meet together in classes and groups for a very good reason: We know that we can learn from one another. Each person is a teacher and a learner. Group discussion of a Bible passage can give us deeper insight into the Word than any of us would have received by studying the passage alone. Out of care for one another in times of joy or difficulty can come an experience of the Christian fellowship that we may not find anywhere else. Out of the shared stories of our individual faith journeys, we can discover deeper faith for all.

The curriculum resources

The United Methodist Church makes available a variety of teaching and learning resources for every age group. These are based on the Bible and follow a plan for lifelong learning and growth. Our teachers use these materials to probe the scriptural basis for the lesson, to plan units and sessions for learning, and to engage students in learning activities. And students use them along with the Bible for direct study, both within class and outside.

Together these four influences provide the basis for a strong biblical faith and a vital discipleship.

For Reflection

1. With others, review the congregation's plan for Christian education: the church school, youth fellowships, vacation Bible school, and other opportunities.
2. Visit a class or group that's new to you. Or help organize a study in an area of special concern.

United Methodist

6 We Minister

To belong to our congregation is to minister to others. In our culture, many people use the word *minister* to mean clergyperson, a pastor or other ordained man or woman. But for United Methodists, all of God's people—children, youth, and adults—are called to be ministers. Most of these people are *laity*—baptized Christians of all ages who minister in formal and informal ways within the church and beyond it.

Two groups of laity who have answered calls to serve in formal ways within the church are deaconesses and diaconal ministers.

- *Deaconesses,* approved by the General Board of Global Ministries and commissioned by a bishop, may be appointed to a servant ministry in any agency or program of the church.
- *Diaconal Ministers,* consecrated by a bishop and accountable to an annual conference, are lay servant leaders who are appointed to a serving profession that embodies both the unity of the congregation's worship and its life in the world.

In The United Methodist Church we have two expressions of ordained clergy, who are also ministers:

- *Deacons:* Men and women ordained by a bishop to a lifelong ministry of Service and Word—especially in leading and supporting baptized Christians in their varied ministries in the world.
- *Elders:* Women and men ordained by a bishop to a lifelong ministry of Service, Word, Sacrament and Order—that is, to serve, preach, teach, administer the sacraments, and order the life of the church for its mission.

Though our gifts vary widely, we're all called to and engaged in the one ministry of Jesus Christ. Some aspects of our ministry are easy and come naturally. Some are difficult, involving long hours, tough work, perhaps with conflict, perhaps with disappointing results. What drives us? What keeps us going? The list includes at least these three things:

- the memory of Jesus' life of service to others, which inspires us to follow him in ministry;
- the assurance of God's gracious love for us, which empowers us to love others;
- the promise of God's coming reign on earth, which draws us into action directed toward this vision.

Let's be more specific. Where does ministry happen?

It happens in our daily activity

For those who are alert to the needs of others, each day abounds with opportunities to serve. We minister with our families as we inquire about one another's lives, as we listen and respond with care, as we touch, as we smile and offer a kind word, and as we decide questions and reconcile conflicts. We take time to listen to a friend in need and we respond; this is often the greatest gift we can offer. We minister at work, to both co-workers and those we serve. We minister in the neighborhood or the shops as we go about the day's work.

It happens through new initiatives

We also go out of our way to minister. We hear of a need, read of a crisis, or see an opportunity to share God's love. It may be with someone across town, someone of another racial or economic group, a person with a disability, or a person of another nation or culture. We take time to call, to visit, to write, and to ask how we can help. We also take the time to respond.

It happens through groups and institutions

Many needs are best met by joining forces with others. We take part in community groups that are trying to serve human need or trying to change social forces that cause suffering. We give our time, our energy, and our money. Though others in these organizations may not think of it this way, for us it's Christ's ministry.

It happens through the church

Through our support and our contributions, we participate in the far-flung ministries of The United Methodist Church—in our district and annual conference, across the nation, and around the world. Here in our congregation we take part in service groups, we sign up for special action projects, we visit, we telephone, we lead, and we teach. And we minister face-to-face in all kinds of ways, both when we gather and in our informal contacts.

Inspired by the example of Jesus and empowered by God's love for us, we all carry out our ministry, both individually and together with others.

For Reflection

1. Have you been involved in any of the four ways in which ministry happens? How?
2. Consider one new ministry that you or your congregation could take on.

7 We Give

To belong to our congregation is to be a steward. Some may say that "stewardship" is just a polite way of referring to financial giving to the church. But it's far more than that.

One character in some of Jesus' parables is the steward—the servant charged by the master to care for the master's property. It is the master, not the steward, who owns the property, but the steward is responsible for it and is accountable to the master. So it is, said Jesus, between God and us. As God's stewards we have three responsibilities:

- *Receiving:* We receive with joyful thanksgiving the many gifts that God showers upon us—time, talent, treasure, our bodies, our friendships, natural resources, and the beauty around us.
- *Managing:* We take good care of what we have received. We manage these resources wisely—for our own good and the good of others.
- *Giving:* Out of our gratitude in receiving so abundantly, we want to share with others.

Let's look at four kinds of gifts that we receive, manage, and share:

Our time

We did nothing to earn the hours, the days, the weeks of our lives. Time is a gift of God. How we choose to use it is a matter of stewardship. Some people lead lives of frenetic activity, always over-extending themselves to the point of exhaustion, while others sit around in apathetic boredom. Some spend all their hours serving the needs of others at the expense of their own, while others live only for themselves.

As Christian stewards we try to manage time wisely and in a balanced way. And we give our time gladly to family and friends, to strangers, to the community, the church, and to ourselves.

Our abilities

Do you remember Jesus' parable of the three servants who received different amounts of money to manage while the master was away? We've each received from God distinctive gifts and talents. How we develop and use these talents is a matter of stewardship. Like two of the servants in Jesus' story, we can invest them wisely—or like the third, out of fear we can hide them (Matthew 25:14-30).

As stewards, we acknowledge the gifts we have without apology. We develop them further, practicing new skills and putting our talents to work in ministry.

Our resources

We may think that our financial resources are our own. But when we recall that the time, the energy, the good health, and the opportunities for employment behind these dollars are all gifts from God, we see that the funds belong to God too. We are the stewards; God is the owner. So questions about what we earn, how we earn it, how we save, spend, and give it away, are all questions of Christian stewardship.

One vital aspect of our stewardship is our giving to Christ's work in the world. We've learned that giving is most effective when we commit ourselves to give a definite proportion of our income through the church. For many, this proportion is one-tenth, or a tithe. Whatever the amount, we have discovered the joy in giving to God the "first fruits," an amount "off the top" of our income, not what's left over at the end of the month.

God's creation

The natural world is also God's gift entrusted to us as stewards. The air, the waters, the soil, native plants and animals, all are part of a biosphere that we share—and which we exploit at our peril. We're called to care for God's creation.

For Reflection

1. List or share with others some difficult choices you have faced in the use of time, ability, and resources. How can the church help?
2. What opportunities for stewardship commitment does your congregation offer? How have you responded? How could you respond?

United Methodist

8 We Organize for Mission

We have said that the mission of our congregation is to reach out and welcome new people; to help them relate to God in Christ; to nurture them in faith and discipleship; and to send them out and support them in their ministry in the world. But for this to happen, we need to be organized. Some people are impatient with organization. They dismiss it as just "church maintenance, busy work, keeping minutes, and wasting hours." But organization is essential to faithful ministry. A structure is needed so we can agree on the direction of our mission, make plans, raise funds, find workers, and do the work of the church.

Our *Book of Discipline* charges every United Methodist congregation to develop a plan for organizing its administrative and programmatic responsibilities (¶ 243). *How* a congregation organizes itself may differ widely from one church to another. Here is a recommended pattern:

Charge conference

The primary governing body of the congregation is the charge conference. This annual meeting of the congregation's leaders is called in advance and chaired by the district superintendent (or a representative). The charge conference adopts goals for the church's mission, reviews and evaluates past work, and elects officers and leaders of the congregation. It may be convened as a *church conference*, where all members of the congregation may attend and vote. However, each congregation must have either a charge conference or a church conference.

Church council

The church council is recommended as the basic program planning and administrative body of the congregation. Between meetings of the charge conference, it provides general oversight and is responsible for the fulfillment of the church's mission. Made up of a chairperson, elected members in several areas (including chairpersons of the four administrative committees listed on the next page), the church treasurer, the lay leader, a lay member of the annual conference, the pastor(s), and others, it is to meet at least quarterly.

There are other schemes for organizing the work of the congregation—for example, the *administrative council* model, or the *administrative board* and *council on ministries* model (in which administrative and programming responsibilities are separated). Still other structures are in use. It's essential that the congregation organizes in a way that allows it to fulfill Christ's mission faithfully.

Administrative committees

All congregations are expected to have the following administrative groups or their equivalent:

- The *committee on lay leadership* keeps track of the congregation's leadership needs. It nominates leaders, who are then elected by the charge conference. The committee is chaired by the pastor.
- The *committee on pastor-parish relations* (or staff-parish relations) works with the pastor(s) and other staff (when employed) to promote open communication with the congregation, develop job descriptions for associate pastors and other staff members, provide annual evaluation, and so forth.
- The *board of trustees* oversees matters related to the property of the local church.
- The *committee on finance* compiles and submits an annual budget to the church council; makes and implements plans to raise enough money to meet the budget; and, through the church treasurer, keeps financial records, makes disbursements, and so forth.

Ministry areas and groups

To faithfully fulfill its ministry, each United Methodist congregation is expected to develop a program of nurture, outreach, and witness. Local congregations have great freedom in how they structure and implement this program. They may elect coordinators of ministry with various age groups (children, youth, adult, family) and chairpersons for ministry areas such as church and society, evangelism, missions, and worship. However, *The Book of Discipline* requires each local United Methodist congregation to have a church school to accomplish the church's educational ministry, as well as to organize units of United Methodist Women and United Methodist Men.

For Reflection

There are many ways to organize for our mission of making disciples. With the help of your pastor or other leader, outline your congregation's plan on the worksheet "Our United Methodist Organization," page 93, Nos. 6-13.

Member's Handbook

9 Our United Methodist Connection

In the early days of the Methodist movement in England, John Wesley recognized the need for communication and accountability. He developed what he called the "connexion:" an interlocking system of classes, societies, and annual conferences. Today we continue this tradition, but our structure is different.

Local church

A congregation is not autonomous. It's part of the United Methodist family and, as such, has certain rights and responsibilities. Through its charge conference it's linked to the district and the annual conference. Its pastor is a member of the annual conference; if other elders are related to the congregation, they, too, are members of an annual conference, as are any deacons. Each year the charge conference elects a layperson or a number of laypeople as members of the annual conference to ensure that the number of lay and clergypersons going to the annual conference is the same. All take part in forming policies and programs that affect the congregation.

District

The district is a division of the annual conference that serves as a link between the congregation and the conference. It's led by a district superintendent ("DS"), an elder appointed by the bishop, usually for a six-year term. The DS oversees the ministry of the district's clergy and churches, provides spiritual and pastoral leadership, works with the bishop and others in the appointment of ordained ministers to serve the district's churches, presides at meetings of the charge conference, and oversees programs within the district.

Annual conference

We use the term *annual conference* in three ways: It's an organizational structure, a geographical area, and a periodic meeting of representatives (the "annual conference session"). As an organizational body, it's made up of ordained members, both active and retired, a number of district and conference leaders, and lay members elected by the charge conferences of all the churches.

It meets at least annually, usually in May or June, to worship and fellowship together, receive reports of past work, adopt goals, programs, and budgets for future work, take stands on key issues, receive new men and women as ordained deacons and elders, and (every four years) elect delegates to Jurisdictional and General Conferences. The bishop of the episcopal area, which may be one or more annual conferences, presides over the annual conference session.

Jurisdiction

In the United States of America, The United Methodist Church is divided into five areas known as jurisdictions: Northeastern, Southeastern, North Central, South Central, and Western. These provide some program and leadership training events to support the annual conferences. Every four years the Jurisdictional Conferences meet to elect new bishops and select members of general boards and agencies.

Central Conference

Outside the United States of America, our denomination is organized according to central conferences. These units—in Africa, Europe, and the Philippines—have their own bishops and delegates to General Conference.

General Conference

Made up of an equal number of clergy and lay delegates elected by annual conferences, the General Conference meets every four years. It's our legislative body, the only organization with authority to speak for The United Methodist Church. It sets our governing procedures (published in *The Book of Discipline*), establishes program emphases, and sets a four-year budget for the church's general work.

We are thankful for the connectional structure of The United Methodist Church; without our connection with other leaders, churches, and resources, our congregation's mission could hardly extend very far.

For Reflection

1. With the help of your pastor or other leader, complete the worksheet, "Our United Methodist Organization," page 93, Nos. 1-5.
2. Consider how your congregation takes part in, and is helped by, each level of the church organization.

United Methodist

10 Our General Councils and Agencies

The basic rules of our denomination are found in *The Book of Discipline of The United Methodist Church*. Revised every four years by the General Conference, the *Discipline* contains our constitution, doctrine, the "Social Principles," and descriptions of how the church is organized at every level. It provides for the following general (church-wide) councils and agencies:

Council of Bishops

Periodically our bishops gather to consult and to study issues in the life of the church and the world, and to call the church to action.

Judicial Council

This "Supreme Court" of our church rules on the constitutionality of the actions of various bodies and officers of the church.

General Council on Ministries

The GCOM oversees the total mission of the denomination. It studies needs for ministry, engages in research and planning, helps to coordinate the programs of various general agencies, and reviews the performance of the general program agencies.

General Council on Finance and Administration

GCFA has a number of financial, legal, and administrative responsibilities. For example, it receives requests for funding from general agencies and develops four-year budgets to propose to the General Conference.

General Board of Church and Society

This program agency, headquartered in Washington, DC, guides the church in responding to social issues that affect the quality of human life. It's a voice of Christian conscience on matters of public policy, but it, like other agencies, cannot speak for the whole denomination.

General Board of Discipleship

Headquartered in Nashville, Tennessee, this board provides resources and services to help congregations make disciples of Jesus Christ—aids that address the deep yearning in the hearts of people to meet and grow in relationship with God. This includes resources of The Upper Room, Discipleship Resources, and the church school curriculum resources.

General Board of Global Ministries

From its New York City headquarters, this program agency oversees the national and worldwide mission of the church, supporting mission programs in hundreds of locations. Its Women's Division relates directly to the work of the United Methodist Women at all levels. And its United Methodist Committee on Relief (UMCOR) helps the whole church respond quickly to emergencies anywhere around the globe.

General Board of Higher Education and Ministry

From its offices in Nashville, this board supports the work of United Methodist schools, colleges, universities, seminaries, and the campus ministry of annual conferences. It guides the preparation of clergy and oversees the work of chaplains, both in the armed services and in institutions such as hospitals and homes.

Other general agencies

- General Commission on Archives and History
- General Commission on Christian Unity and Interreligious Concerns
- General Commission on Communication (United Methodist Communications)
- General Board of Pension and Health Benefits
- General Commission on Religion and Race
- General Commission on the Status and Role of Women
- General Commission on United Methodist Men
- The United Methodist Publishing House

We support the work of many of the above agencies through our congregation's budget, part of which goes to the World Service Fund, as it's called. When we take our vows of church membership, we become a part not only of our congregation but also of The United Methodist Church as a whole. Together we accomplish for Christ what we could not do alone.

For Reflection

1. For a deeper understanding of the general boards and agencies of The United Methodist Church, read *The United Methodist Primer: 2001 Revised Edition* by Chester E. Custer, Chapter Eleven: "The Local Church and Its Connections."
2. In the next weeks and months, take a look at *The Book of Discipline of The United Methodist Church—2004*, Chapter Five, pages 451-670, and Chapter Seven, especially pages 709-716.

Member's Handbook

11 We Belong to the Whole Church

To be a member of this congregation is to belong to something much larger than a denomination. It's to be part of Christ's body—a church that transcends the centuries and includes people of all cultures, all nations, and all denominations.

We're brothers and sisters with Catholic peasants in Bolivia, Russian Orthodox worshipers in St. Petersburg, the Christians still struggling with divisive issues in South Africa, and believers in a small house church in Shanghai.

We claim to be part of an "ecumenical" church. The word *ecumenical* comes from the Greek word meaning "the inhabited world." It's used to indicate Christ's whole church—his whole Body of followers around the globe.

But this Body really is not "whole," is it? We can see that it's broken in many ways—through conflict among nations, races, classes, denominations, and even among Christians of the same denomination. We confess this brokenness and ask God's forgiveness. We search for ways to reach across barriers, unite with other Christians, and find answers to the problems that divide us. Here are a few of the ways:

Joining with other Methodists

The United Methodist Church is only one of many members of a worldwide Methodist family. The family includes Methodist denominations of other nations that have sprung out of missionary efforts—churches that have since become autonomous. It includes various churches of the Wesleyan tradition that became divided from one another in past years over matters of creed, social practice, or race.

For example, in the United States of America, we're closely allied with three sister denominations composed largely of African-American Methodists: The African Methodist Episcopal (AME) Church, The African Methodist Episcopal Zion (AME Zion) Church, and the Christian Methodist Episcopal (CME) Church.

Some seventy-four Methodist denominations join hands through The World Methodist Council, headquartered at Lake Junaluska, North Carolina. With more than 36 million members, these Wesleyan bodies worship and work in 130 countries around the planet. Every five years, delegates meet to celebrate our common Wesleyan heritage and address world issues together.

Working and worshiping with other traditions

Another way we have of expressing our ecumenical unity is to worship together with those beyond the Methodist family and to work with them in serving people in need or changing unjust practices. This may be as simple as asking a neighboring Presbyterian church to join in a common service on Thanksgiving Day or as complex as forming a church coalition to address alcohol and drug abuse in the community.

We do not need to agree on every matter of belief or ritual to come together in Christ's name. And in so doing we take small steps toward healing Christ's broken body.

Serving through ecumenical councils

In addition, we seek ways to link with other denominations on a continuing basis. One way is through councils at various levels, representative bodies for dialogue, fellowship, worship, and joint work; for example, local councils or clergy associations, the Consultation on Church Union (COCU), the National Council of Churches of Christ in the USA, and the World Council of Churches.

As we think and act as faithful members of the whole body of Christ, we contribute to the healing that Christ so earnestly desires: "that they may become completely one, so that the world may know that you have sent me and have loved them even as you have loved me" (John 17:23).

For Reflection

1. Review the ways your congregation works with churches beyond the United Methodist family.
2. Think of other opportunities that could be developed.

United Methodist

Part Two:

We Remember

Can you remember the house where you lived at age five? Can you recall the face of your first love? Do you occasionally bring to mind the joy of a child's birth or the pain of a loved one's death?

In a sense, you *are* what you remember. Today's experience is part of a long river of experience extending from the past into the present and on into the future. One of the ways you affirm yourself is by recalling and retelling your life story.

So it is with the church. To be a member of our congregation is to stand in a long stream of history. It's to recall and retell our special story, beginning with the ancient Hebrews and continuing to this very day, and even into the tomorrows that lie ahead. The more familiar we become with this story the more we sense that it's truly *ours*. We begin to feel that we were there with Abraham and Sarah, Moses, Naomi and Ruth, Jeremiah, Jesus, Paul, Luther, the Wesley brothers, Barbara Heck, Francis Asbury, Otterbein, Albright, and more.

Why are we so interested in this story? It's because we see in it the guiding activity of God. Across the centuries and around the world, men and women have opened themselves to God's Spirit. Some have run from God, or rebelled, or deliberately disobeyed. But others have confronted the greatest challenges, even death itself, in a courageous and faithful spirit. From our past we learn what God expects of us today, and we receive vivid images of what being faithful is all about.

In this section we can barely touch on a few of the highlights of our history. But it may be enough to remind us of its extraordinary power. To belong to the church is to remember this story.

12 Our Jewish Roots

In the second millennium B.C., a Semitic tribal group came to settle in and around the Jordan valley, an area called Canaan then, later Palestine, and now roughly equivalent to the state of Israel. As the centuries passed these Hebrews, as they called themselves, came to see that they had been chosen by God for a special relationship. This came to involve at least seven features:

God of all

God was revealed to the Hebrews or Israelites as holy, single, indivisible. "Hear, O Israel: The LORD is our God, the LORD alone" (Deuteronomy 6:4). Though others might believe in several gods, for the Hebrews God was whole and one. And eventually they came to know this one God not only as their own tribal deity but also as the Lord of all peoples and of all creation.

Covenant

The Israelites also came to recognize that God had called them into a special relationship: a two-way promise or a *covenant.* The Lord would be their God and would provide them land and descendants; they would be faithful to the Lord and keep the commandments. Often this stiff-necked people broke the covenant, but again and again they were forgiven and the relationship with God restored.

Liberation

The pivotal event of the Israelites' history was their liberation by God from bondage in Egypt. Under Moses this ragtag band of ex-slaves organized themselves into a sojourning nation and received the Law from God. And after forty years, God led them into the land that had been promised to their ancestors.

Law

The people's obligations of faithfulness were codified as laws—for example, what we know as the Ten Commandments. More elaborate laws were developed, and the first five books of the Bible became known as the Law, or the Torah. It was a compilation of what the believer must do to be seen as just in the eyes of God.

Prophecy

Between 800-600 B.C., a number of prophets, such as Isaiah, Amos, and Jeremiah, spoke in vivid terms of what God was doing in the social and religious events of their times. Often their word was of God's judgment on present practices and a warning of dire consequences unless the people reformed. Sometimes it was a word of hope in God's deliverance from present suffering.

Expectation

Around 1000 B.C., under the kings Saul, David, and Solomon, the Hebrew nation had a shining hour, but the following centuries saw disunity, foreign occupation, and exile. Sustained by the covenant, prophets foretold a coming day of salvation. By the time of Jesus' birth, when Palestine had been occupied by Rome for some sixty years, many Jews were expecting that God's Anointed One, or Messiah, would soon appear to lead them into a brighter future.

Tension

But there was little agreement among the Jews, for they were divided into several parties: the Pharisees (strict keepers of the law); the Sadducees (supervisors of the worship at the Temple in Jerusalem); the Zealots (militantly anti-Rome, ready for an armed rebellion if a new David would lead them); and the Essenes (a small monastic community in the wilderness).

This long-ago story of the Hebrews is our story as well. Why? Because the roots of our faith are here. And it was here in this tradition that our Lord was born and nurtured; here he ministered, died, and rose from the dead; here the early church first flourished. We claim continuity with our Jewish past—their story is our story too.

For Reflection

1. Consider your sense of kinship with our Jewish forebears. Do you feel that this is your story as well?
2. How could you identify with it more fully?

United Methodist

13 Jesus

Jesus is the heart of all that we are as a church, all that we believe and do as Christians, and our very life as forgiven, renewed, and whole persons. What are the essential points of his life and ministry? (For our doctrine of Christ, see topic 33.)

Baptism

Jesus was reared in Nazareth of Galilee in the northern part of Palestine. The oldest son of Mary, he may have followed his earthly father Joseph's trade as a carpenter. But in his middle adult years he became a traveling teacher. His baptism by John at the Jordan River seems to have been a crucial turning point. There he experienced God's Spirit descending upon him, and he heard the voice of God (Matthew 3:16-17).

Temptation

Jesus was then led by the Spirit into a wilderness, where he fasted. He struggled with several kinds of temptation but rejected them, and he returned with a clearer sense of his mission.

Disciples

Like other teachers of the time, he gathered a band of disciples, twelve men who followed him and strove to understand his teachings. They were an undistinguished lot and slow to comprehend who Jesus was. But they were to become the nucleus of the Christian church.

Ministry

Jesus was a rabbi, or *teacher*, interpreting the Scriptures to all who would listen. He taught with authority: "You have heard that it was said…. But I say to you…" (Matthew 5:27-28). And he taught with vivid imagination, using figures of speech and parables that were unforgettable.

Jesus was also a *preacher*. His basic message was, "The kingdom of God has come near; repent, and believe in the good news" (Mark 1:15). That is, the promised time of God's reign is coming very soon; turn from your unrighteous ways and put your trust in the promises of God's love.

Jesus was also a *healer*. Many came with illnesses, both physical and mental. Some saw his extraordinary gift for healing as a "sign" of his divine nature.

Messiah

It appears that at first Jesus wanted to keep his special relationship with God hidden. But when Peter proclaimed, "You are the Messiah" (Mark 8:29), Jesus did not deny it. The Hebrew word *Messiah* was translated into Greek as *Christ;* both terms mean the Anointed One, chosen and confirmed by God.

Conflict

As Jesus' identity became clearer, his troubles with the religious parties increased. The Pharisees began opposing Jesus because he attacked their self-righteous efforts to keep the Law and because he was more concerned with the spirit of the Law than the letter of the Law. The Sadducees opposed him because he did not support their temple religion. The Zealots could not support Jesus, for he had no interest in throwing off the Roman yoke through violence. Although Jesus knew that these parties were strongest in Jerusalem, he resolved to go there to celebrate the Passover.

Passion and death

In Jerusalem, at a final supper with his disciples, Jesus asked them to remember him later in the breaking of bread and drinking of wine. Meanwhile, the Sadducees were bringing their grievances to the Roman governor Pontius Pilate, who reluctantly ordered Jesus' execution. After a time of mocking and torture, he was crucified by Roman soldiers on Golgotha, a hill outside the city.

Resurrection

On the first day of the week, our Sunday, some of the women who followed Jesus discovered his grave empty and were astonished to meet him alive! Other disciples were incredulous, but shortly many of them also met the living Christ. He commissioned them to go and make disciples of all nations, to baptize and teach others (Matthew 28:19-20), to feed his lambs and tend his sheep (John 21:15-17). And he promised that they would receive power when the Holy Spirit came (Luke 24:49).

For Reflection

1. Consider what qualities of Jesus draw you to him. Write down the words that would describe the difference Jesus has made in your life.
2. Share your experience of Jesus with another.

Member's Handbook

14 The Church Is Born

After Christ's resurrection, some of his followers continued to meet and pray in Jerusalem, awaiting the promised Holy Spirit. Little could they imagine the astonishing events that would follow in that first century A.D.!

Pentecost

On Pentecost, a Jewish holy day fifty days after Passover, the disciples were gathered in an upper room. There, with the sound like a violent wind and tongues as of fire, "All of them were filled with the Holy Spirit" (Acts 2:4).

They rushed out and began to speak "in other languages," such that some in the crowd thought they were drunk. But Peter proclaimed that it was not wine but the Holy Spirit that was responsible. He went on to preach the first sermon of the church, attesting to the wonders and signs that Jesus did, his death and resurrection, and his messiahship—and some three thousand people were baptized (Acts 2:5-42). Thus, Pentecost became the birthday of the church.

Peter

Jesus had given Peter his name—*Peter* means "the rock" in Greek—and said that "on this rock I will build my church" (Matthew 16:18). It seemed an unlikely prediction: Peter would fall asleep in the Garden of Gethsemane while Jesus was praying, and before the night was out he would deny his Master three times. Yet Peter became the central figure of the new church in Jerusalem. Though for a while he was not willing to open the church to Gentiles (non-Jews), through a compelling revelation he came to see that God shows no partiality, but in every nation anyone who fears him and does what's right is acceptable to him (Acts 10:34).

Paul

Saul of Tarsus in Asia Minor (Turkey today) was a devout Jew, "the son of a Pharisee" and a Roman citizen himself. Saul was threatened by the new Christians, so he volunteered to work for the Sadducees in persecuting them. But on his way to Damascus he was confronted by the Risen Christ, blinded, and later nurtured by Christians in Damascus. He converted to the new faith, and his sight was restored.

From then on Saul, now known as Paul, devoted his remarkable energies to missionary work, traveling throughout the eastern Mediterranean, establishing small Christian churches in several cities, then keeping in touch with them by letters. It's Paul who proclaimed the central tenet of our salvation—that we're saved, not by our own works, but by God's loving, forgiving grace known through our faith in Jesus the Christ.

The Holy Spirit

Though the early Christians did not yet have a clearly formed doctrine of the Trinity, they had no doubt as to the source of their extraordinary power and growth: It was God's living Spirit among them, the Spirit Jesus had promised.

The Holy Spirit was particularly evident in the calamitous days of persecution later in the century. As the Christian community grew, Rome began to view it as a threat to emperor worship and public order. The emperors, Nero (beginning in A.D. 64) and Trajan (A.D. 98), undertook cruel campaigns against Christ's followers. Many were lost, but the Spirit used the death of martyrs to strengthen the church.

The written Word

Paul's letters were copied and circulated among the churches, as were letters by others. Around A.D. 70, Mark wrote a brief, action-packed account of the good news of Christ—the first "Gospel." Many other Gospels were written and shared, some better than others. As the first century closed, the beginnings of our New Testament were taking shape. And here, too, we affirm, the Holy Spirit was at work, inspiring devoted disciples to write the saving truth of Jesus the Christ, God's Word.

For Reflection
1. Read again the story of Pentecost in Acts 2.
2. Ponder the role of God's Spirit in creating and leading the early church.

United Methodist

15 The Roman Church

By the second century the church had entered a new period. It was firmly established around the eastern Mediterranean Sea, but there was little agreement on beliefs or organization.

The Church Fathers

Several influential leaders wrote widely in an effort to clarify the faith and to define the orthodox view. The church grew, and its theology became more certain. But it was still a time of persecution. A number of the patriarchs of the second and third centuries were martyred for their faith: Ignatius, Polycarp, Justin, Cyprian.

Perhaps the most influential of all the Fathers was Augustine, born in A.D. 354 in what is now Algeria. After an undisciplined adolescence, he was converted and became a Christian theologian, teacher, writer, and bishop of Hippo. We know him best for two of his works, *The Confessions* (about his early life and conversion) and *The City of God* (on good and evil).

State religion

Before Augustine a dramatic change had occurred in the Christian world. In the year A.D. 312 the Roman emperor Constantine professed the Christian faith, and by the end of the century Christianity had become the religion of the Roman state. Two cities of the empire, Rome and Constantinople (today's Istanbul, in Turkey), became the centers of the rapidly growing church. By A.D. 395 pagan worship had been outlawed, and the Roman Empire was divided into two realms. The church remained unified until the eleventh century, when it split into Roman Catholicism in the West and Eastern Orthodoxy—a schism that has never been healed.

The Bible

Between the years A.D. 200 and A.D. 400, Christian leaders wrestled with the question of which writings were to be regarded as truly apostolic, that is, written by one of the original apostles or on their behalf. About A.D. 200 a list was developed in Rome that had twenty-two of our twenty-seven New Testament books and some others. Other lists were also proposed. Finally, the canon of twenty-seven books was adopted at a council of church leaders in Hippo in A.D. 393 and in Carthage in A.D. 397 (both in North Africa).

By then Christians had already agreed that the Hebrew Scriptures were to be regarded as an integral part of the Christian canon. Thus, Jerome's Latin translation, completed in A.D. 405, included the sixty-six books of our Holy Bible.

The medieval church

After the fall of Rome in the fifth century, the church was the major institution tending the lamp of learning and civilization. It provided a link with the past, as monks copied ancient Greek and Latin manuscripts, secular as well as Christian. It was the primary patron of the arts, eventually prompting an astonishing renaissance of sublime architecture in church and cathedral building. It was the center of intellectual activity, establishing the first universities, which would stimulate a flowering of learning as the Middle Ages came to an end.

Through it all the church gained exceptional power over all aspects of life, and often it was closely allied with political power. By definition, all persons in Europe were Roman Catholic Christians, and the church controlled their belief and action. But there was immorality among religious leaders; there was a blatant display of church wealth in a poor society. As the new era of enlightenment dawned in the fifteenth and sixteenth centuries, Roman Catholic authority was increasingly challenged. Change was in the air.

For Reflection

1. Evaluate Constantine's establishment of Christianity as the state religion. How did this affect faith?
2. Are there any vestiges of state religion in the United States of America today?
3. In your view, what's the proper relationship between church and state?

Member's Handbook

16. The Reformation

Late in the Middle Ages the winds of dissent were blowing in many quarters of the Roman Catholic Church. In the sixteenth century, especially in northern Europe and Britain, these winds gathered into a hurricane of protest, reform, and eventual splintering of the church. This protest took different forms.

Luther

Born of German peasant parents in 1483, Martin Luther grew to be an intensely disciplined and studious young man. Renouncing worldly comforts, he became an Augustinian monk and later a professor of biblical literature at the university in Wittenberg. He proclaimed several principles that were at odds with his Roman tradition.

- *Justification by faith:* Our salvation is not through our own merit or any works we can perform, but solely by God's unmerited grace, through our faith in Christ.
- *Priesthood of all believers:* Each Christian is able to communicate directly with God and is responsible to do so. Further, we are priests to one another: We are Christ one to another, doing to our neighbor as Christ does to us.
- *Primacy of Scripture:* The Bible, not the tradition of the church, is the primary authority for Christian faith and life, and, thus, is to be studied by all believers. This led to the printing of Bibles in the language of the people and widespread education so that it could be read.

Though Luther set out only to reform the Roman church, the gulf widened. Fueled by the political ambitions of the German rulers, the split with Rome was complete by 1530.

Zwingli and Calvin

At the same time, Huldreich Zwingli was preaching reform in Zurich, Switzerland. He rejected the Catholic use of images, incense, and candles, turning church buildings into simple, unadorned meeting places.

These concerns were expressed more fully in the movement initiated by John Calvin, a French theologian living in Geneva. In 1536 he published the *Institutes of the Christian Religion,* a systematic doctrinal basis for Protestant churches. Believing in the predestination of certain "elect" persons to be saved by God, the Bible-centered, sober-living Calvinists grew in number.

Anabaptists

Among the more radical sects were the Anabaptists, who concluded that baptism of infants was invalid because the newborn were not capable of belief. They were split by different Bible interpretations; many were persecuted and even executed.

The Church of England

In Britain, where our Methodist roots lie, the Reformation took a different turn. There were various early dissenters from Rome, but it was the king's political ambition that turned the tide. When Pope Clement VII refused to grant King Henry VIII a divorce, the monarch had his own Archbishop of Canterbury do the job. For this, the pope excommunicated the king, so Henry retaliated. In 1534 he rejected papal authority and declared the monarch the head of the church in England, a decree that's still in effect today. King Henry also dissolved the monasteries and confiscated their property.

Under Queen Elizabeth I in the late sixteenth century, the Anglican Church continued as a unique blend of Roman Catholicism and Protestantism. Among those who desired a more thorough reformation of the church were the Puritans. Though they grew in number and strength, their efforts were quashed in the early seventeenth century, and thousands fled to New England. Even today the Church of England seems Roman in some ways but Protestant in others.

For Reflection

1. The results of the Reformation are still with us. What would you say were the positive outcomes? The negative?
2. Looking back a few generations, in what divisions of the church does your own family background lie? What strengths were brought from each tradition?

United Methodist

17 John Wesley

For the vast working class, the early eighteenth century was dismal in England. The Industrial Revolution had brought long hours of drudgery at low pay, while the relative few lived in increasing luxury. The Church of England provided little comfort. Too often it served the powerful and rich; it was formal and ritualistic, with little attention given to personal piety, discipline, Bible study, prayer, or serving the needy. Into this environment came a man God would use to work a major change, the founder of the Methodists, John Wesley.

Student

Wesley was born in 1703, the fifteenth of nineteen children of Samuel and Susanna Wesley. Samuel was the rector (priest) of the Anglican parish church at Epworth, some 150 miles north of London. Susanna was a strong woman, intelligent and pious, who managed the household with strict discipline and provided the early schooling for each child.

At age eleven John was sent to school in London and at seventeen to Oxford University. He studied for the priesthood, was ordained at twenty-five, and later returned to teach at one of the colleges. There his brother Charles and other students had started a small group for religious study and discipline, and soon John became its leader. Ridiculed for their strict ways, the members were called "the Holy Club," "the Bible-Moths," "the Methodists." But the group continued to meet, to visit the jails, and to take food to the sick and poor.

Missionary

Although intensely serious about religion, John did not sense an abiding faith in Christ. Thinking missionary work might help, he and Charles sailed to the coast of Georgia to work with settlers and Native Americans there. But the trip turned out to be a disaster. John's rigid ways and an abortive romance caused ill feelings; following Charles, he returned to England a discouraged man. One benefit of the experience, however, was his introduction to the quiet assurance of faith shown by the Moravians, a sect based in Germany.

On May 24, 1738, John Wesley's life changed. At a Christian gathering on Aldersgate Street in London, while listening to the reading of Luther's Preface to Paul's Letter to the Romans, he felt a remarkable assurance of faith: "I felt my heart strangely warmed. I felt I did trust in Christ, Christ alone for salvation." Though John hardly mentioned this "Aldersgate experience" again, it seems to have released him for an incredibly passionate and productive ministry over the next five decades.

Preacher

John Wesley began preaching the good news of Jesus Christ wherever he could. Because his message was so personal and the response so enthusiastic, the Anglican authorities became alarmed; and one parish church after another was closed to him. But that didn't stop him, for as he proclaimed, "I consider the world as my parish." Traveling on horseback, he covered some 250,000 miles in his lifetime.

Writer

Wesley was a prolific author: sermons, books, pamphlets—he even edited a magazine for a time. He wrote almost daily in his journal, a candid account of his own spiritual struggles, the ups and downs of the new Methodist movement, and his adventures on the road. Though he wrote a number of hymns, some of which are in our *Hymnal*, his brother Charles was the master, composing and publishing thousands of hymns. It was largely due to Charles that the Methodists became a singing people and still are.

Organizer

Through the Wesley brothers thousands came to know Christ as their Savior, but these converts needed the support of one another to maintain their commitment. John organized and managed a nationwide "connexion" of classes, societies, and annual conferences, through which believers were held accountable to God by one another. Without this closely knit organization and Wesley's active leadership of it, the revival he sparked could have simply faded away.

For Reflection

1. You may want to read the account of Wesley's Aldersgate experience. It's found in Albert C. Outler (ed.), *John Wesley* (New York: Oxford University Press, 1964), pages 51-69.
2. Did you know that Wesley's practice of forming "classes" and "societies" for the sake of accountable discipleship continues in United Methodist churches to this day? Ask your pastor about Covenant Discipleship. Or, for more information, contact the General Board of Discipleship of The United Methodist Church at (615) 340-1765 or www.gbod.org.

Member's Handbook

18 John Wesley's Legacy

Wesley never left the Church of England; he had hoped to reform it from within. He did not intend to launch a new denomination, and late in life he discouraged his followers from doing so. But it has been said that when he died at age eighty-seven, he left behind "one silver spoon, a worn-out clergyman's coat, a much-abused reputation, and…the Methodist Church."

In part, his remarkable legacy was a strong organization of classes, societies, and annual conferences, which did indeed become a church after Wesley's death. In part, his legacy was a passionate faith and a spiritual energy that the Church of England had not seen before. Perhaps most of all, he left a balanced and sensible way of believing, one that incorporated the best from many traditions but avoided the extremes. Here are some examples:

Both Scripture and tradition

Like Luther and the other Reformers, Wesley put primary emphasis on the Scriptures. He read the ancient languages, studied the Bible daily, used biblical texts as the basis of every sermon (and it sometimes seems, in every sentence!). Yet, like the Catholics and Anglicans, he also honored the long tradition of the Christian church. In matters of belief he kept Scripture and tradition in balance.

Both faith and works

Like Luther, he held up faith in Jesus Christ as the sole avenue of salvation. Nothing we may do or say can earn God's favor. But unlike Luther, John Wesley did not diminish the importance of Christian works. He believed that grace and faith empower us for works of love, for acting out our faith in Christian discipleship. He and his followers served the poor, the prisoner, the widow, and the orphan. Faith and works could not be separated.

Both gospel and law

In Wesley's time some Christians were saying that the gospel was all that mattered. They held that keeping the law by living a righteous life according to God's commands was unnecessary, for we're saved by grace through faith. Others argued that only acts of piety and righteousness were needed. Wesley rejected both extremes. Both gospel and law were necessary. In fact, he would emphasize one or the other, depending on his audience. To the downtrodden, disillusioned, and contrite, he preached the gospel of grace; to the self-satisfied sinners he preached God's judgment under the law.

Both experience and reason

Many of the free churches that were springing up in Wesley's time put major emphasis on Christian experience, one's direct and often emotional encounter with the renewing power of the Holy Spirit. At the other extreme was the prevailing philosophy of deism, a very rational, impersonal way of thinking about God. Wesley claimed we need both experience and reason, both emotion and intellect. Much of the response to his preaching was personal, even emotional. But he insisted on more than that; careful study of the Bible and thoughtful discussion of theological issues were essential.

Both Word and sacrament

The Reformers majored in preaching, believing that in the interpretation of Scripture, God's Word was heard afresh. Some even abandoned the sacraments, seeing them as trappings of a corrupt Roman church. Wesley could not accept this. Both the preached Word and the sacraments were necessary means of grace. Though a preacher through and through, he took Holy Communion in an Anglican church several times a week and encouraged all the Methodists to do so.

Today United Methodists strive diligently to maintain the balanced way of believing and practicing the Christian faith that John Wesley has left them. They thank God for this legacy.

For Reflection

1. What aspects of John Wesley's legacy do you value most?
2. What evidence of Wesley's life and work are apparent in your congregation? Are there Wesleyan emphases that seem to be missing?

United Methodist

19 Methodists in the New World

The Wesleyan revival was centered in England, but by the mid-eighteenth century it was spreading into Scotland and Ireland—and soon to the American Colonies. Here are some key elements in the story of American Methodism:

Robert Strawbridge

A strong-willed Irish lay preacher named Robert Strawbridge emigrated to northern Maryland. By 1766 he was preaching the Methodist message, and later he apparently organized a Methodist society. He even went so far as to administer the sacraments of baptism and Holy Communion, later a matter of contention with the Methodist clergy. He traveled throughout Maryland and parts of Virginia, planting Methodism wherever he went.

Barbara Heck and Philip Embury

Meanwhile, other immigrants from Ireland settled in New York. There Barbara Heck stirred her cousin Philip Embury to resume his role as a Methodist class leader and lay preacher. In the fall of 1766 the society was founded that was to become John Street Methodist Episcopal Church, our oldest congregation. For a time the society met in a rigging loft. Here the group was frequently led by a new recruit, the colorful British Captain Thomas Webb, who preached in full military uniform with his sword on the pulpit!

Francis Asbury

In 1768 a New York member wrote John Wesley to appeal for more experienced leadership. Several English volunteers responded, including Francis Asbury, an earnest layman who was twenty-six years old when he answered the call in 1771. He rapidly became the outstanding leader of the Methodists in America and helped to establish the circuit rider pattern for preachers. In forty-five years he traveled 270,000 miles on horseback and on foot, preaching over 16,500 sermons!

The Christmas Conference

Wesley initially opposed the American Revolution. But after the events leading to the colonies' independence from Britain, his attitude changed, and he resolved to help strengthen Methodist work in the newly formed

United States of America. Believing that he had the right to ordain, he consecrated Thomas Coke as a "general superintendent" of Methodist work in America, with instructions to consecrate Asbury in the same office. When Coke arrived in America, Asbury declined to accept the office without an election by the other preachers.

So on Christmas Eve 1784, nearly sixty of the eighty-one Methodist preachers gathered in Baltimore at the Lovely Lane Chapel for a special conference. Here they agreed to form an independent church, The Methodist Episcopal Church. Francis Asbury, still a layman, was ordained a deacon on Christmas Day, an elder the next day, and general superintendent (along with Coke) the next! Four years later the title changed to *bishop*.

The Christmas Conference also adopted an order of worship, a liturgy for the sacraments, a system of discipline, and a statement of doctrine called the Articles of Religion. It passed resolutions on the emancipation of slaves, an establishment of a college, and the sending of missionaries to Nova Scotia. A new church had been born, even before there was a Methodist church in Britain.

Expansion

Methodist work expanded rapidly. Asbury continued his travels, from New York to Tennessee. He was much like Wesley—a firm, dominant, committed, and beloved patriarch. He gave form to the new office of bishop. He demanded that preachers not settle in the more comfortable cities but move with the people into the rural frontiers. Thomas Coke also traveled widely, often with Harry Hosier, a lay, African-American evangelist, whom Coke called "the best preacher in the world." While Coke preached to a packed house inside, Hosier would address the overflow crowd outside.

For Reflection

1. What factors do you think were responsible for Methodism's success in America?
2. Which of these strengths do our churches still retain?

Member's Handbook

20 Philip William Otterbein

In addition to our roots among the early Methodists of Britain and America, there are two other denominational sources of today's United Methodist Church. One of these is a German-speaking church born in Pennsylvania. Its founder was Philip William Otterbein.

Student, teacher, pastor

Born in Germany in 1726, Philip was the son of John Otterbein, rector of the local Latin School and a preacher in The German Reformed Church. Philip began his college education at Herborn Academy in Germany, where there was strong emphasis on disciplined living and the mission of the church. After graduation he taught school, then returned to Herborn, where he became a teacher in the Academy. Ordained in 1749, he preached and held prayer meetings regularly. But his preaching was too intense for some parishioners, who asked the church authorities to either restrain the young pastor or to remove him. The authorities refused to do either.

Missionary to America

In the mid-eighteenth century, there were perhaps 90,000 German-speaking people living in Pennsylvania. A representative of the Dutch Reformed Church there appealed to Herborn Academy for missionaries. Philip was one who agreed to go, leaving for America in 1752.

For six years Philip Otterbein served as pastor of a German Reformed Church in Lancaster, Pennsylvania. There, during a time of spiritual depression, he prayed fervently for the grace about which he had been preaching to others. He came to an inner assurance that was a turning point in his ministry. From then on he preached about the need to experience God's forgiveness. He served other parishes and married a member of one, Susan LeRoy.

"We are brethren!"

Probably in 1767, while serving as a pastor at York, Pennsylvania, Otterbein attended a service in a barn in Lancaster County. There he heard the Mennonite preacher Martin Boehm speak of his spiritual struggle and an experience of Christian assurance like Philip's. At the end of the sermon Otterbein threw his arms around Boehm and exclaimed in German, *"Wir sind Brüder!"* ("We are brethren!"). From then on, the two men were close friends and worked together in revitalizing their churches.

In 1774 Otterbein went to serve the German Reformed Church in Baltimore. Actually, he refused the invitation at first, but a Methodist friend, Francis Asbury, urged him to come. Later he would attend the Methodist Christmas Conference and take part in the consecration of Asbury.

United Brethren in Christ

At a gathering in 1800, some lay preachers who looked to Otterbein for guidance adopted the name "United Brethren in Christ." At that conference Otterbein and Boehm, who had been expelled from the Mennonite church, were elected superintendents and later bishops. The loosely organized body continued to expand its work on the eastern seaboard, Appalachia, and west into Ohio and Kentucky.

The Methodists and United Brethren in Christ had very similar beliefs and organization. Sometimes preachers from both groups would witness together, one preaching in English, the other in German. The one group was often called the "English Methodists" and the other called the "German Methodists."

Philip Otterbein died in 1813 at age eighty-seven, still a pastor of the Reformed Church. Francis Asbury responded to the news by saying, "Is Father Otterbein dead? Great and good man of God!"

For Reflection

1. Describe the parallels and differences between Philip Otterbein's life and John Wesley's.
2. The "inner assurance" of God's grace was a turning point for each man. What is the place of such assurance in your own journey of faith?

United Methodist

21 Jacob Albright

There was another "German Methodist" group, whose founder was Jacob Albright. Born in 1759 near Pottstown, Pennsylvania, Jacob was the son of immigrant German parents and became a member of The Evangelical Lutheran Church.

The honest tilemaker

At age twenty-six he married Catharine Cope and bought a farm in Lancaster County, Pennsylvania. There, in addition to farming, he set up a kiln to manufacture tile and bricks. So conscientious was he that he was known as "the honest tilemaker."

But in 1790 several of the Albright children died in an epidemic. Jacob had been fairly indifferent toward religion, but now he turned for help to a German Reformed pastor and two lay preachers, Methodist and United Brethren. It was a dark time in his life.

"I was converted."

At a prayer meeting the next summer Albright poured out his heart to God, confessed his unworthiness, and found a spiritual awakening. "Gradually every anguish of heart was removed, and comfort and the blessed peace of God pervaded my soul…. I was converted deep into eternal life." With this rebirth he turned to the Methodists, and before long he was made a lay preacher and encouraged to travel as a circuit rider. With limited command of the English language, he turned more and more to German-speaking people.

Traveling preacher

Soon Jacob was preaching in Pennsylvania, Maryland, and Virginia—in churches, homes, barns, and schoolhouses, in the woods and in open fields. He had a blunt manner and emphasized life-changing Christian experience, such that people of the more established churches often felt threatened. Some accused him of neglecting his family; indeed, Catharine herself was not too happy with his long absences.

But people responded to Albright's preaching in growing numbers. They were an ardent group, often ridiculed as fanatics. Like the Methodists, Albright brought together classes and appointed class leaders. In an 1802 conference of these classes, they declared themselves to be a church. Five years later, at the church's first annual conference, Jacob Albright was named bishop. Though it had no formal Methodist ties, the new denomination called itself "The Newly-Formed Methodist Conference."

By this time Albright's health was in decline. He continued to preach and supervise the classes, but in 1808 he died of tuberculosis, aggravated by his exposure to the elements as a traveling preacher. He was only forty-nine.

The Evangelical Church

In 1816, the church took a new name, The Evangelical Association, which was changed later to The Evangelical Church. For many years these "Albright People" were closely allied to the "Otterbein People," both German Methodist bodies. But it was not until over a century later, in 1946, that they united as a single denomination: The Evangelical United Brethren Church. It's this body that joined with The Methodist Church in 1968 to form a new denomination: The United Methodist Church.

To be a United Methodist today is to be an heir of these three American churches—Methodist, United Brethren, and Evangelical—all intensely personal in their faith and zealous in evangelistic outreach.

For Reflection

1. Our founders—John Wesley, Philip Otterbein, and Jacob Albright—all went through a period of personal darkness followed by a spiritual awakening or a conversion. Consider the importance of conversion for our church, then and now.

2. Have you experienced your own time of personal darkness and conversion? Think about where you are currently in your spiritual journey and how our founders' experiences give us hope in the dark times in our faith.

Member's Handbook

22 The Nineteenth Century

In the nineteenth century, "the people called Methodist," both English-speaking and German, played a crucial role in the nation's growth and its push to the West. Six forms of ministry were especially prominent.

Circuit riders

Many preachers were appointed to ride the circuit, a loop of small frontier communities, often hundreds of miles around. The preacher preached, distributed literature from his saddlebags, helped to establish new congregations, and brought news of the world. It was not an easy life. The salary at one point was set at $64 a year, and almost half of the preachers died before they were thirty years old.

Camp meetings

Early in the century a new religious form appeared, the annual camp meeting. Settlers from miles around would come with their wagons and tents, staying for a week or so. Evangelistic preachers of several denominations would stand on stumps or special platforms, proclaiming a vivid and emotional call to repentance and acceptance of God's grace. The often electrifying response brought many conversions and spread a vast spiritual revival across frontier America.

Sunday schools

The Sunday school was instituted in England in the late eighteenth century to teach poor children to read, to teach the Christian faith, and to teach morals. Wesley adopted it for the Methodists, and in nineteenth-century America it spread rapidly. In congregations that were visited by a preacher only once in several weeks or months, the Sunday school was the chief means for Christian learning. Though called a school, the purpose was largely evangelistic. In the latter part of the century, Methodists joined with other denominations in the cooperative development of lessons for all ages.

Publishing

The Americans followed Wesley's practice of distributing Christian literature, especially needed with the widely scattered population. In 1789 The Methodist Book Concern was founded to keep the circuit riders supplied with literature. The Evangelicals named a book agent in 1816. Later, the Evangelical Press and Otterbein Press served the two German-speaking churches. From these small beginnings the publishing enterprise has grown into The United Methodist Publishing House, located in Nashville.

Missions

Thomas Coke, whom Wesley sent to America, is often called the father of Methodist missionary outreach. He challenged the church to share the gospel with others, and in 1804 the Methodists named him general superintendent of all missions. The Missionary Society of the Evangelical Association was formed in 1839.

One of the outstanding missionaries to Native Americans was John Stewart, an African-American preacher among the Wyandot people of the Midwest. The first Methodist missionary abroad arrived in Liberia in 1819. Work in China and India began at mid-century. By the late nineteenth century, missionaries were at work around the globe, with strong support from American congregations, Sunday schools, young people's groups, and women's organizations. New congregations were established, as well as countless hospitals, clinics, schools, colleges, and orphanages.

Schools

In the United States of America the church was also at work founding schools and universities. The Methodist General Conference of 1820 urged annual conferences to develop colleges; by 1850 a number were functioning, many of which endure today. There are now 123 colleges, universities, seminaries, and professional and secondary schools with United Methodist ties.

For Reflection
1. How have these ministries—camp meetings, Sunday school, publishing, missions, and so forth—touched the lives of your ancestors?
2. How is your life touched by these ministries today?

United Methodist

23 Division and Reunion

The process of fracturing Christ's church over differences in belief and practice, which had begun in the Reformation, continued through much of the nineteenth century. Our American forebears experienced division, time and again.

Methodist divisions

As early as 1792 a conflict arose over the question of the bishops' authority, and some preachers withdrew to form The Republican Methodist Church.

In 1816 experiences with racism caused Richard Allen and others to pull away to form The African Methodist Episcopal (AME) Church. In a further split five years later, The African Methodist Episcopal Zion (AME Zion) Church was formed.

In the 1820's a group of Methodists sought the rights for stronger lay leadership in the church. But they were unsuccessful and left in 1830 to become The Methodist Protestant Church.

In the 1840's disagreement over the slave issue grew. When southern delegates blocked General Conference discussion, dissident abolitionists withdrew to form The Wesleyan Methodist Church. Polarization over slavery at the 1844 General Conference led to a Plan for Separation. In 1845 The Methodist Episcopal Church, South, was organized by delegates from southern annual conferences, leaving The Methodist Episcopal Church to serve the north and west.

The Free Methodist Church was organized in 1860. And after the Civil War another African American denomination, The Colored (now Christian) Methodist Episcopal (CME) Church, began in 1870.

During the 1890's small holiness sects split off from the Methodist churches, some of which united as The Church of the Nazarene in the early twentieth century. Others were absorbed in the Pentecostal movement.

United Brethren and Evangelical divisions

In 1889 a majority of The United Brethren Church wanted a new constitution, an altered Confession of Faith, and lay membership in General Conference. A minority dissented and left the fold to organize The United

Brethren Church (Old Constitution), which still remains a separate denomination. The Evangelical Church divided two years later in 1891. The majority continued as The Evangelical Association, while a minority formed The United Evangelical Church in 1894.

Reunion

Early in the twentieth century a new tide was sweeping across the church. Christians believed that God was calling them to heal Christ's broken body. This ecumenical movement took many forms. One result was that sister churches once divided began to talk about reunion. In 1922 the two branches of The Evangelical Church reunited, and in 1946, at Jamestown, Pennsylvania, it joined with The United Brethren Church as the new Evangelical United Brethren (EUB) Church.

The Methodist Church

In 1939 in Kansas City, Missouri, three major Methodist branches came together—The Methodist Protestant Church; The Methodist Episcopal Church, South; and The Methodist Episcopal Church. The new denomination simply was called The Methodist Church. However, to reach agreement the delegates compromised on the racial issue; they created six jurisdictions in the church—five geographical areas and a sixth for African Americans. The "union" was not complete.

The United Methodist Church

In 1968, at a joint General Conference in Dallas, The Evangelical United Brethren Church and The Methodist Church came together to form The United Methodist Church (with no racial jurisdictions). Each branch brought its special gifts from the rich legacy of the Wesleys, Otterbein, Albright, and our other founders.

For Reflection

1. Do you believe the Holy Spirit works in both division and reunion?
2. Do you think further union of the United Methodists with other bodies would be useful? Faithful? Why or why not? With what groups?

Member's Handbook

24 A Church of Many Colors

Though we call ourselves *United Methodists,* we're certainly not uniform Methodists. In fact, we're perhaps one of the most diverse denominations in the world! Now and then our differences cause problems. We do not see eye to eye on every issue. But in general, we find our diversity a rich blessing.

Global differences

The connectional system of the United Methodist denomination links members of many nations and cultures all across the world. Currently, there are seven central conferences organized in Africa, Europe, and the Philippines. In the United States, United Methodist churches are grouped into five regional jurisdictions. The many perspectives of our worldwide church are represented when the jurisdictions and central conferences are asked to elect the members of our national agencies and to send representatives to our General Conference.

Economic differences

We sometimes think of some denominations as serving largely wealthy members, while others appeal more to blue-collar workers. We United Methodists seem to attract a broad economic spectrum (with some concentration of the middle class in the United States). The variety of members of the United Methodist denomination throughout the world enhances our ministries.

Theological differences

We also represent a broad spectrum of Christian beliefs. There are a number of issues on which we would find different positions even within a single congregation: the virgin birth, the miracles, the physical resurrection of Christ, the authority of the Bible. We sometimes use labels to describe our differences—liberal, conservative, liberationist, evangelical, feminist—but such names in themselves are not helpful.

When we're at our best, we respect our differences and use them to the church's advantage. We speak clearly and listen with understanding. We acknowledge our various perspectives but seek common ground for common action.

Ethnic differences

In some congregations people of various races and cultures are worshiping, learning, and serving together. More often, our ethnic diversity is found in our districts and conferences, or in national or global settings where representatives of various ethnic congregations gather. What a beautiful rainbow we make!

In the United States there are many cultures represented in our United Methodist churches:

United Methodists who are Native American enrich our whole church with distinctive reverence for the land, our home, and the Spirit that guides us.

United Methodists who are Hispanic American—a rapidly growing group—bring a depth of spirit that enlivens the church wherever they are.

United Methodists who are Asian American include Japanese, Chinese, refugees from Southeast Asia, and an expanding Korean population.

United Methodists who are Pacific Islander—including Tongans, Samoans, and Fijians—offer another hemisphere of experience.

United Methodists who are African American bring a special perspective on social justice and human dignity. Their heritage, experience, and commitment increase our sensitivity to God's will for our time.

United Methodists who are Caucasians of widely varied European backgrounds, most of them now far removed from the "immigrant" identity, also contribute diverse gifts to the community of believers.

When these ethnic groups are added to the many cultures represented in The United Methodist Church across the globe, our ethnic richness is clearly visible.

Our unity in Christ

We have our differences, which often seem to make life more complicated. But we're certain that we do not want a world or a denomination in which everyone is just alike. We rejoice in our church of many colors, nationalities, and cultures, and we celebrate our allegiance to one God, a faith that transcends all differences. "So we, who are many, are one body in Christ, and individually we are members one of another" (Romans 12:5).

For Reflection

1. Consider some of the differences discussed in this section as they're found in your congregation and in your area.
2. In what ways have these differences been a problem?
3. In what ways have they enriched Christian faith and discipleship?
4. How has your congregation been involved in learning more about The United Methodist Church in other parts of the world?

United Methodist

25 Into the Future

We've seen that to be a member of the church is to remember the past. We recall our origins in the ongoing dialogue among God and the men and women of faith throughout the ages.

But why? We remember because this is our story. These are *our* mothers and fathers in the faith, and we're their heirs. Without them we would not be who we are. So we remember them to honor them and give thanks.

But there's another reason. We remember our past to guide our future. From past centuries of struggle, of controversy and suffering and martyrdom, of conscientious witness and loving ministry, emerge the guidelines for our own faith and discipleship as we become the church of tomorrow. As The United Methodist Church moves into the future, what hopes do we have? Consider these five hopes.

Faithfulness

We intend to "keep the faith." Whatever may come, we resolve to remain faithful to God as revealed in Jesus Christ. And not only to *keep* the faith but to *share* it. We know the faith is always only one generation removed from potential extinction. We will share the good news with the coming generation and with all who will receive it.

Near the end of his life, John Wesley shared a vision of the future: "I am not afraid that the people called Methodist should ever cease to exist either in Europe or America. But I am afraid lest they should only exist as a dead sect, having the form of religion without the power. And this undoubtedly will be the case, unless they hold fast both the doctrine, spirit, and discipline with which they first set out." We intend to "hold fast."

Growth

In recent years The United Methodist Church, along with most other mainline Protestant denominations, has been suffering a decline in membership. The analysts point to several causes: a more secular and urban society, less caring congregations, dull worship services, the needs of many people for rigid codes and beliefs, and so forth. Whatever the causes, we want to reverse this trend. We intend to draw new people into faith and into our congregation. We intend to become a growing church again.

Diversity in unity

We resolve to be "one body with many members." We will accept, respect, and celebrate our differences. We will listen to all and use the contributions of all. But we will remain one Body, united in Christ and in one another.

Ministry

We intend to love, to care, to minister. We will "be there" with others. Our world is wounding its people in many ways. Millions near and far are hurting physically, mentally, and spiritually. But we believe that Jesus Christ is there suffering with them, ministering to them—and we resolve to join him.

Transformation

We believe that God is now at work transforming the world, moving it closer to the day of *shalom,* to the time of God's reign of peace promised of old. We see the church as a sign, a lively demonstration of the nature of this coming kingdom. We live in expectation of *shalom.* We open our lives to Christ's renewing power. We join God in this global transformation by working to change the systems and institutions that now degrade, exploit, and divide people. We support the works of peace, justice, reconciliation, beauty, love, and joy.

The story of Christ's church through the ages is not only our story, it's also now in our hands. In times to come, what will people remember about these years when we were the ones responsible for Christ's work?

For Reflection

1. To what extent do you join in the hopes for our future? Describe a few specific actions you and your congregation could take to realize these visions.
2. If your congregation has a long-range plan, study it to see where you fit in.

Member's Handbook

Part Three

We Believe

*B*elonging...remembering...believing. To be a full member of the church involves all three. When it comes to believing, what's your own story? Do you think of yourself as "a believer?" Do you belong to the "community of believers," as we call the church? Have you had times of serious doubt or unbelief?

Actually, there are two kinds of believing, and both are essential for Christian life. They're closely related and influence each other, but they're different. One is *belief* and the other, *beliefs.* One is *faith* and the other, *doctrine* or *theology.*

Faith. Faith is the basic orientation and commitment of our whole being—a matter of heart and soul. Christian faith is grounding our lives in the living God as revealed especially in Jesus Christ. It's both a gift we receive within the Christian community and a choice we make. It's trusting in God and relying on God as the source and destiny of our lives. Faith is believing in God, giving God our devoted loyalty and allegiance. Faith is following Jesus, answering the call to be his disciples in the world. Faith is hoping for God's future, leaning into the coming kingdom that God has promised. Faith-as-belief is *active;* it involves trusting, believing, following, hoping.

Theology. Theology or doctrine is more a matter of the head. It's thinking together in the community of believers about faith and discipleship. It's reflecting on the gospel. It's examining the various beliefs we hold as a church. Some may say that theology is only for professional theologians. This is not true. All of us, young and old, lay and clergy, need to work at this theological task so that our beliefs will actually guide our day-by-day actions and so that we can communicate our belief to an unbelieving world.

As a church member you're called to believe; that is, called to both belief and beliefs, to be faithful and to think theologically. But you may sometimes feel like that father who cried out to Jesus, "I believe; help my unbelief!" (Mark 9:24). For those of us whose belief is unfinished or unsteady, help is on the way. Our congregation is just the sort of place where faltering belief can be strengthened. And God is there as well: "the Spirit helps us in our weakness" (Romans 8:26). Paradoxically, when faith is weak we can turn to the Holy Spirit, who will lead us another step along the way.

May your study and discussion of this section help you move onward in the journey of believing.

26 Our Faith Journey

What's the bedrock of life for Christians? Is it Bible reading? Church participation? Prayer? Is it a belief that Jesus is God's Son?

The foundation of Christian living is faith in Christ. Faith is the central loyalty that gives purpose and direction to our lives. Christian faith is grounding our lives in the living God as revealed especially in Jesus the Christ.

This faith does not happen overnight. It's a journey. From birth to death we're growing in faith. There are ups and downs—and sometimes long flat stretches where we seem to be stalled in our journey. But little by little, most of us deepen our relationship with God.

In part, this growth in faith is a *gift*. Through our participation in the community of faith, through our openness to God's love, we receive this marvelous treasure. But faith is also a *choice* we make, an often difficult decision to put God and God's reign first in our lives, no matter what the cost.

We cannot say that some people are "ahead" in the journey of faith and others "behind." Faith is not something we possess by degrees. The journey is complex, different for each traveler, and involving at least four intertwined pathways:

Trusting

First and foremost, faith is trusting. To be a person of faith is to rely on God, to know that "the Lord is my shepherd" (Psalm 23). It's to rest confidently in the power and care of the living, loving Lord who's revealed in the Bible and in our own experience. Faith is to give ourselves to the movement of God's Spirit in our lives and in our times, not knowing where it will lead. To trust God is to "strive first for the kingdom of God and his righteousness" (Matthew 6:33) and to put all other trusts in a secondary position.

Believing

Faith is also believing *in* someone. In the Apostles' Creed, for example, we say, "I believe in God the Father Almighty, maker of heaven and earth." This is not the same as saying, "I believe *that* God the Father Almighty exists." Rather, we're confessing our confidence in God, our devoted loyalty, and our allegiance. Such belief may involve going beyond what we're sure of and taking a "leap of faith."

Following

There's more to faith than trusting and believing. Faith is more active, a matter of *doing* as well as *being.* So Jesus said to his first disciples, "Follow me." To be faithful is to follow Jesus the Christ. It is to be one of his disciples, seeking to understand his will and his way—and to do it. Such discipleship is not an easy matter. Jesus said, "If any want to become my followers, let them deny themselves and take up their cross and follow me. For those who want to save their life will lose it, and those who lose their life for my sake will find it" (Matthew 16:24-25). To be people of faith is to set aside anything that might weaken our daily discipleship.

Hoping

Christian faith is also a matter of hoping, of leaning into the future that God has promised. It's living with the assurance that God is bringing in the time of *shalom,* God's reign here on earth. As Easter people we have a hope born of the Resurrection: God has already conquered sin and death, and the kingdom of love, righteousness, peace, and justice is even now breaking in. To abide in this hope is to watch and pray for God's future and to join in the ministries through which it will be realized.

Surrounded by the love and encouragement of the community of believers, we persevere on the journey of faith, ever trusting, believing, following, and hoping.

For Reflection

1. Recall some of the mountains and valleys of your own faith journey and the plateaus. Describe them on paper or share them with a Christian friend.
2. In which of the pathways of faith are you growing? In which do you seek further growth?

United Methodist

27 Our Theological Journey

Interwoven with our faith journey is a theological journey, a lifelong adventure of working out our beliefs. Theology is thinking together about our faith and discipleship. It's reflecting with others in the Christian community about the good news of God's love in Christ.

Both laypeople and clergy are needed in "our theological task." The laypeople bring understandings from their ongoing effort to live as Christians in the complexities of a secular world; clergy bring special tools and experience acquired through intensive biblical and theological study. We need one another.

But how shall we go about our theological task so that our beliefs are true to the gospel and helpful in our lives? In John Wesley's balanced and rigorous ways for thinking through Christian doctrine, we find four major sources or criteria, each interrelated. These we often call our "theological guidelines": Scripture, tradition, experience, and reason. (See *The Book of Discipline of The United Methodist Church—2004,* pp. 76-82.) Let's look at each of these.

Scripture

In thinking about our faith, we put primary reliance on the Bible. It's the unique testimony to God's self-disclosure in the life of Israel; in the ministry, death, and resurrection of Jesus the Christ; and in the Spirit's work in the early church. It's our sacred canon and, thus, the decisive source of our Christian witness and the authoritative measure of the truth in our beliefs.

In our theological journey we study the Bible within the believing community. Even when we study it alone, we're guided and corrected through dialogue with other Christians. We interpret individual texts in light of their place in the Bible as a whole. We use concordances, commentaries, and other aids prepared by the scholars. With the guidance of the Holy Spirit, we try to discern both the original intention of the text and its meaning for our own faith and life.

Tradition

Between the New Testament age and our own era stand countless witnesses on whom we rely in our theological journey. Through their words in creed, hymn, discourse, and prayer, through their music and art, through their courageous deeds, we discover Christian insight by which our study of the Bible is illuminated. This living tradition comes from many ages and many cultures. Even today Christians living in far different circumstances from our own—in Africa, in Latin America, in Asia—are helping us discover fresh understanding of the gospel's power.

Experience

A third source and criterion of our theology is our experience. By *experience* we mean especially the "new life in Christ," which is ours as a gift of God's grace; such rebirth and personal assurance gives us new eyes to see the living truth in Scripture. But we mean also the broader experience of all the life we live, its joys, its hurts, its yearnings. So we interpret the Bible in light of our cumulative experiences. We interpret our life's experience in light of the biblical message. We do so not only for *our* experience individually but also for the experience of the whole human family.

Reason

Finally, our own careful use of reason, though not exactly a direct source of Christian belief, is a necessary tool. We use our reason in reading and interpreting the Scripture. We use it in relating the Scripture and tradition to our experience and in organizing our theological witness in a way that's internally coherent. We use our reason in relating our beliefs to the full range of human knowledge and in expressing our faith to others in clear and appealing ways.

For Reflection

1. Explore how Scripture, tradition, experience, and reason contribute to a specific Christian belief, such as our doctrine of the Holy Spirit.
2. When engaging in theology, which guideline are you most likely to overlook? How can you remedy this?

Member's Handbook

28 The Congregation Supports Our Journey

We've seen that "belief" and "beliefs"—faith and theology—are not the same. Faith is grounding our lives in the living God as revealed especially in Jesus the Christ. Theology is thinking together about our faith and discipleship.

Though we must each take responsibility for our own journey along these interrelated pathways, we do so within the community of believers. In our congregation all of us need help, and all can offer help. How do we support one another in our journeys of faith? Here are seven ways:

Through baptism and confirmation

Whether we're baptized as infants, youth, or adults, baptism is our initiation into the body of Christ and a crucial step in our journey of faith. And whether our profession of faith happens at the same time, or later (as with infant baptism), baptism is a decisive moment of faith commitment. In both cases we're surrounded by the congregation's love and upheld in our further growth. The next two topics deal with baptism, confirmation, and profession of faith.

In conversation

We help one another by simply communicating. We pay attention to one another and listen. We take the courage to speak what's in our hearts. We are not afraid to raise profound concerns with one another—loneliness, doubt, confusion, anger, pride, and hope. Even when we don't know the "religious" words, we try to answer out of the depths of our faith. In this way, faith and theology grow.

In suffering and joy

We help one another take steps along the way at times of crisis or fulfillment. When serious illness strikes a friend or family member, we find ways to care; and in caring, talk may turn to matters of faith. When death comes, we share our grief and our confidence in God's unending love. In disappointment, despair, victory, or accomplishment, Christian friends can help one another grow.

In celebration

In our congregation's service of worship, as nowhere else, we're in touch with the church's tradition. The Scripture is read and interpreted. Through the witness from the pulpit we're challenged to receive God's gift of faith, to take new steps in trusting, believing, following, hoping. In hymn and liturgy and creed we celebrate our journey together. In Holy Communion, in special Advent and Lenten services, in weddings and funerals, we take further steps toward deeper belief and stronger beliefs.

In study

The church school and other study groups provide opportunities for us to help one another along the path. Here we may focus on study of the Bible; with the help of teachers and resources, we find that the Scripture speaks to our faith and informs our theology. The same is true when study focuses on some aspect of the church's tradition.

In decision

We also help one another grow in faith and sharpen our doctrine as we confront difficult decisions together. These may be issues regarding the church's life and work, faced in committee or board meetings or by the entire congregation. Often before the right direction can be found we must answer again questions about who we are and whose we are. We may be pushed to new depths of faith; we may need to stretch to new levels of theological understanding.

In ministry

Likewise, as we engage in ministries of witness, service, and action in the community or wider world, we're learning faith and theology. In fact, some of us may grow most significantly by first rolling up our sleeves and plunging into active ministry, then later stopping to reflect on it from the perspective of faith.

In all these ways and more, our participation in the congregation supports and guides the Christian journey each of us is making.

For Reflection

1. Describe ways your journey of faith and theology has been enriched by your participation in the congregations you have known.
2. What additional support do you need now?

United Methodist

29 We Are Baptized

United Methodists believe in the baptism of people of any age: infants, children, youth, and adults. No matter what age, the sacrament makes a profound difference in our journey of faith.

Sacrament

Along with most Protestant churches, we practice two sacraments: baptism and Holy Communion. A sacrament is a special act of worship that was *instituted by Christ* and is a *means of God's grace.* The ritual acts point to God's presence in the created world (even in such ordinary things as water, bread, and wine) and are means to convey God's love and to transform us. No, sacraments do not have magical power; but they're channels through which God makes grace available to those who will receive it.

The baptismal covenant

We read in Matthew's Gospel that Jesus was baptized by John (Matthew 3:13-17) and that he commanded his disciples to baptize in the name of the Father, Son, and Holy Spirit (28:19). In Acts we see that from the day of Pentecost on, baptism was the gateway into the new church (2:37-42).

In The United Methodist Church we speak of our ritual as a service of the "Baptismal Covenant." (See *The United Methodist Hymnal,* pp. 32-54.) That is, as part of the enduring covenant between God and the church, a new three-way covenant is established between the person being baptized, the community of believers, and God.

By water and the Holy Spirit

Water is the central symbol of baptism. It links us with our biblical story and suggests a cleansing of sin. In our church the water may be administered by sprinkling, pouring, or immersion; each has its symbolic values.

But from New Testament times baptism has been by water *and the Spirit.* In our service of baptism, following the water baptism the pastor and others lay hands on the baptized person and invoke the Spirit's work, that "you may be a faithful disciple of Jesus Christ."

The meaning of baptism

Based on the early church's experience and John Wesley's emphases, we recognize four intertwined meanings in this sacrament:

- *Incorporation into the body of Christ:* Baptism is our initiation, our incorporation into the body of believers. Whether infant, youth, or adult, from then on we're "baptized members" of the church—of Christ's whole church, of The United Methodist Church, and of the local congregation.

- *Forgiveness of sin:* In our baptism God offers to wash away our sin, to heal our separation, and to restore us to a right relationship. As youth or adults, we respond by accepting this forgiveness; with infants, the parents or sponsors promise to teach about the church and nurture the child's faith so that he or she will be ready later to profess his or her own faith.
- *New life:* Baptism is a sign of the new birth we receive through the Holy Spirit. In it we celebrate the death of our old nature and our entry into new life in Christ. The *personal experience* of new birth—also called regeneration—may or may not coincide with baptism itself. In fact, we should take care not to equate regeneration with the moment we become conscious of it. It is better to think of regeneration as a process that grows out of God's grace and takes our entire lives to complete.
- *Doorway to holy living:* Therefore, baptism also marks the beginning of our growth in grace through which we come closer to Christ, deepen our love for God and neighbor, and approach that "holiness of heart and life" that was Wesley's standard.

The congregation's part

Baptism is not an individual sort of thing. Through baptism we're incorporated into the body of Christ as represented by the congregation. Therefore, baptism is a solemn act of worship and commitment by the congregation because it assumes responsibility for the nurture of the newly baptized person. As baptized members, we now live out our baptismal vows within the ongoing, nurturing life of the whole congregation.

The age at baptism

Some denominations hold that baptism is not appropriate until a person is able to understand what's happening and can make an informed choice for the Christian way. United Methodists baptize infants and children primarily because of their understanding of God's grace. At baptism the child is given the gift of the Holy Spirit; as church members nurture, love, and provide for the child, they act as channels through which the Spirit brings God's transforming grace to the child.

For Reflection

1. Study and discuss the service of "The Baptismal Covenant I" in *The United Methodist Hymnal*, pages 33-37, parts 1 through 11.
2. Share the meaning of your own baptism in your journey of faith.

30 We Profess Our Faith

In addition to the sacrament of baptism, there are other rites through which we celebrate stages in our journey of faith and in our relationship to Christ's church.

Confirmation

Particularly for those who have been baptized as infants or children and, thus, have not had an opportunity to profess their faith publicly, United Methodists offer the service of confirmation. Many confirmands are youth between the ages of eleven and fourteen, who have been nurtured in faith in the years since their baptism, and who now respond to God's grace with intentional commitment. A period of deliberate preparation is offered. Peers who have not yet been baptized may participate in the preparatory classes.

But confirmation is not "joining the church." It's not a "completion of baptism." Baptism is complete in itself; through it, we're initiated into the church. In confirmation we remember our baptism, figuratively speaking, and the fullness of its four meanings (outlined in the previous section). We profess our faith in the midst of the worshiping congregation. Through the ritual act of laying on of hands, the Holy Spirit "confirms" (strengthens, makes firm) the faith we've professed. And the congregation pledges its continued support.

In confirmation the "baptized member" of the church becomes a "professing member" of the congregation, The United Methodist Church, and the universal church. (And he or she is now included in the reckoning of "church membership" for statistical purposes.)

Profession of faith

Unbaptized youths or adults who have come to the point of faith in Christ and who wish to be received into the church, of course, cannot "remember their baptism." They have never made their baptismal vows, so the time has come for them to affirm these vows as part of their baptism. For them the service of baptism and profession of faith is one act; no separate rite of confirmation is needed.

Just as confirmands do, candidates for profession of faith need careful instruction in the meaning of baptism and in the teachings and practices of the Christian faith and The United Methodist Church. They will also enter the church as "professing members" and will be upheld in faith by the congregation.

Transfer of membership

Those who are already baptized members of another denomination of Christ's church and who wish to transfer their membership to a United Methodist congregation simply take a vow of loyalty to The United Methodist Church and pledge faithful participation in our congregation's ministries, "by your prayers, your presence, your gifts, and your service."

Persons transferring from another United Methodist church simply take the vow of participation. In either case, the congregation responds by welcoming them and by renewing its own covenant of faithful participation. (See *The United Methodist Hymnal,* p. 38.)

Reaffirmation of our profession of faith

In our journey of faith, times may come when a sense of God's leading is more clear and compelling than ever. Now and again someone with a fervent renewal of faith will think, "I want to be baptized again." But there's no such thing as a second baptism. For each of us, baptism is once and for all.

Yet we all need to take part in acts of spiritual renewal within the faith community. In part we do this every time the congregation participates in a baptism. In addition, from time to time we may join in a "Congregational Reaffirmation of the Baptismal Covenant," in which we again renounce our sin, profess our faith, give thanks for what God has done, and pledge our faithful participation in the church's ministries. (See *The United Methodist Hymnal,* pp. 50-53.)

For Reflection

1. If you're preparing to be received into the church, discuss with your pastor the meaning of this step and the liturgy to be used.
2. Take time to study the vows of membership you will be expected to take. See, for example, the appropriate sections of "The Baptismal Covenant I," *The United Methodist Hymnal*, pages 33-39.

United Methodist

31 We Believe in God

The Christian life is, in part, an adventure in learning to entrust our lives to God. From the days of infancy, as we begin to sense that the people around us are trustworthy, until the last breath of life is taken with faith in God's unending love, we're learning to ground our lives in God.

But it is a mystery, isn't it? We cannot fully define this faith, much less define God. Though we meet God, we cannot capture the nature of God in words. Still, it's important to work at our "theological task," using the Scripture, the church's tradition, our own experience, and our reason. What words shall we use to speak of God?

Who God is

When we say the Apostles' Creed, we join with millions of Christians through the ages in an understanding of God as a Trinity—three persons in one: Father, Son, and Holy Spirit. From early in our Judaic roots we've affirmed that God is one and indivisible, yet God is revealed in three distinct ways. "God in three persons, blessed Trinity" is one way of speaking about the several ways we experience God.

We also try to find adjectives that describe the divine nature: God is transcendent (over and beyond all that is), yet at the same time imminent (present in everything). God is omnipresent (everywhere at once), omnipotent (all-powerful), and omniscient (all-knowing). God is absolute, infinite, righteous, just, loving, merciful...and more. Because we cannot speak literally about God, we use metaphors: God is a Shepherd, a Bridegroom, a Judge. God is Love or Light or Truth.

What God does

We cannot describe God with certainty. But we can put into words what God *does* and how we experience God's action in our lives. God works in at least these seven ways:

- *God creates.* In the beginning God created the universe, and the Creation is ongoing. From the whirling galaxies, to subatomic particles, to the unfathomable wonders of our own minds and bodies—we marvel at God's creative wisdom.
- *God sustains.* God continues to be active in creation, holding all in "the everlasting arms." In particular, we affirm that God is involved in our human history—past, present, and future.

- *God loves.* God loves all creation. In particular, God loves humankind, created in the divine image. This love is like that of a parent. We've followed Jesus in speaking of God as "our Father," while at times it seems that God nurtures us in a motherly way as well.
- *God suffers.* Since God is present in creation, God is hurt when any aspect of creation is hurt. God especially suffers when people are injured. In all violence, abuse, injustice, prejudice, hunger, poverty, or illness, the living God is suffering in our midst.
- *God judges.* All human behavior is measured by God's righteous standards—not only the behavior itself but also the motive or the intent. The Lord of life knows our sin—and judges it.
- *God redeems.* Out of infinite love for each of us, God forgives our own self-destruction and renews us within. God is reconciling the individuals, groups, races, and nations that have been rent apart. God is redeeming all creation.
- *God reigns.* God is the Lord of all creation and of all history. Though it may oftentimes seem that the "principalities and powers" of evil have the stronger hand, we affirm God's present and future reign.

When all is done, if we have difficulty in imagining who God is or in relating to God, there's a simple solution: *Remember Jesus*—for in the New Testament picture of Jesus, we see God.

For Reflection

1. Try making a list of names and metaphors for God, your own as well as those of other believers.
2. Give examples of God's action in each of the seven areas listed.

Member's Handbook

32 We Confess Our Sin

Genesis 1:27 asserts that we've been made in the image of the Creator. Like God we have the capacity to love and care, to communicate, and to create. Like God we're free, and we're responsible. We've been made, says Psalm 8, "a little lower than God" and crowned "with glory and honor." We believe that the entire created order has been designed for the well-being of all its creatures and as a place where all people can dwell in covenant with God.

But we do not live as God intends. Again and again we break the covenant relationship between God and us. We turn our backs on God and on God's expectations for us. We deny our birthright, the life of wholeness and holiness for which we were created. We call this alienation from God, *sin.*

A distinction should be made between sin and sins. We use the word *sins* to denote transgressions or immoral acts. We speak of "sins of omission and commission." These are real enough and serious, but they're not the essential issue.

The issue is *sin* in the singular. Sin is our alienation from God, our willful act of turning from God as the center of life and making our own selves and our own wills the center. From this fundamental sin our various sins spring. Sin is estrangement of at least four kinds:

Separation from God

Sin is breaking the covenant, separating ourselves from the One who is our origin and destiny. It's trying to go it alone, to be out of touch with the God who is the center of life. Based on the story in Genesis 3, the church has described this break in dramatic terms: *the Fall.*

Separation from other people

In our sin we distance ourselves from others. We put ourselves at the center of many relationships, exploiting others for our own advantage. Instead of loving people and using things, we love things and use people. When confronted with human need, we may respond with token acts of kindness or with lip service or perhaps not at all. Toward some people and some groups, we're totally indifferent or actively hostile. Sin is a denial of our common humanity and our common destiny on this one small planet.

Separation from the created order

In our sin we separate ourselves from the natural environment. Greedily we turn upon it, consuming it, destroying it, befouling it. As natural resources dwindle, as possibilities increase for long-term damage to the atmosphere and seas, we pause to wonder. But our chief concern is for our own survival, not for the beauty and unity of all God's creation.

Separation from ourselves

We turn even from our own center, from the goodness, happiness, and holiness that is our divinely created potential. Sometimes it seems that there are two wills warring within us. As Paul put it, "I do not understand my own actions. For I do not do what I want, but I do the very thing I hate" (Romans 7:15).

Paul continues: "Wretched man that I am! Who will rescue me from this body of death?" (Romans 7:24). Like Paul, we discover that we are powerless to extricate ourselves from sin. Though we work ever so earnestly at various means of saving ourselves—being good, going to church, reading the Bible—these in themselves cannot save us. Sin is not a problem to be solved. It's our radical estrangement from God, a separation that only God can heal by a radical act of love. We yearn for this reunion, this reconciliation, this redemption, this salvation.

For Reflection

1. Reflect on the difference between sin and sins. Consider how some particular sins with which you're familiar are rooted in sin, the separation from God.
2. How does Paul's lament in Romans 7:15 and 24 speak to you?

33 We Believe in Jesus the Christ

In an earlier section of this handbook (topic 13), we remembered the life, ministry, death, and resurrection of Jesus. As Christians we believe *that* these events occurred. But we also believe *in* Jesus the Christ. We trust him and we follow him. We bring him our allegiance and confident devotion. We rest our hopes on him.

In trying to find words to express their faith in Jesus, the New Testament writers gave him various names. Jesus was Master, Rabbi, Teacher. He was the Way, the Truth, and the Life. He was the Doorway to the sheepfold, the Light of the world, the Prince of Peace, and more. In the church's long tradition, scores of other names or titles have been given. Let's look at five of the most central biblical names for Jesus:

Son of God

We believe in Jesus as God's special child. We call this the *Incarnation,* meaning that God was in the world in the actual person of Jesus of Nazareth. The Gospel writers explain this in different ways. In Mark, Jesus seems to be adopted as God's Son at his baptism. In Matthew and Luke, Jesus is conceived by the Holy Spirit. In John, Jesus is God's pre-existing Word who "became flesh and lived among us" (1:14). However this mystery occurred, we affirm that God is wholly present in Jesus Christ.

Son of man

Paradoxically, we also believe that Jesus was fully human. One of the church's first heresies claimed that Jesus only *seemed* to be human, that he was really a divine figure in disguise. But the early church rejected this. It affirmed that Jesus was a person in every sense that we are. He was tempted. He grew weary. He wept. He expressed his anger. In fact, Jesus is God's picture of what it means to be a mature human being.

Christ

We say "Jesus Christ" easily, almost as if "Christ" were Jesus' surname. Yet this name is another way of expressing who we believe Jesus to be. *Christ* is the Greek translation of the Hebrew word *Messiah,* which means God's Anointed One. For years before Jesus' time the Jews had been expecting a new king, a descendant of the revered King David, who would restore the nation of Israel to glory. Like kings of old, this one would be anointed on the head with oil, signifying God's election; hence, the Chosen

One = the Anointed One = the Messiah = the Christ. The early Jewish Christians proclaimed that Jesus was, indeed, this Chosen One. Thus, in calling him our Christ today, we affirm that he was and is the fulfillment of the ancient hope and God's Chosen One to bring salvation to all peoples, for all time.

Lord

We also proclaim Jesus as our Lord, the one to whom we give our devoted allegiance. The word *Lord* had a more powerful meaning for people of medieval times, because they actually lived under the authority of lords and monarchs. Today some of us may find it difficult to acknowledge Jesus as Lord of our lives. We're used to being independent and self-sufficient. We have not bowed down to authority. To claim Jesus as Lord is to freely submit our will to his, to humbly profess that it is he who is in charge of this world.

Savior

Perhaps best of all, we believe in Jesus as Savior, as the one through whom God has freed us of our sin and has given us the gift of whole life, eternal life, and salvation. We speak of this gift as the *atonement*, our "at-oneness" or reconciliation with God. We believe that in ways we cannot fully explain, God has done this through the mystery of Jesus' self-giving sacrifice on the cross and his victory over sin and death in the Resurrection.

For Reflection

1. What names for Jesus are most meaningful for you and why?
2. In just a few sentences state your own belief in Jesus. Share this with others.

34 We Are Saved

What does it mean to be saved and to be assured of salvation? It's to know that after feeling lost and alone, we've been found by God. It's to know that after feeling worthless, we've been redeemed. It's to experience a reunion with God, others, the natural world, and our own best selves. It's a healing of the alienation—the estrangement—we've experienced. In salvation we become whole.

Salvation happens to us both now and for the future. It's "eternal life," that new quality of life in unity with God of which the Gospel of John speaks—a life that begins not at death, but in the present. But how does salvation happen?

By grace through faith

Salvation cannot be earned. There's no behavior, no matter how holy or righteous, by which we can achieve salvation. Rather, it's the gift of a gracious God.

By *grace* we mean God's extraordinary love for us. In most of life we're accustomed to earning approval from others. This is true at school, at work, in society, even at home—to a degree. We may feel that we have to act "just so" to be liked or loved. But God's love, or grace, is given without any regard for our goodness. It's unmerited, unconditional, and unending love.

As we come to accept this love, to entrust ourselves to it, and to ground our lives in it, we discover the wholeness that God has promised. This trust, as we've seen, is called *faith*. God takes the initiative in grace; but only as we respond through faith is the change wrought in us.

This is the great theme of the Protestant Reformers, as well as John Wesley and the Methodists who followed: We're saved by grace alone through faith alone. We're made whole and reconciled by the love of God as we receive it and trust in it.

Conversion

This process of salvation involves a change in us that we call *conversion*. Conversion is a turning around, leaving one orientation for another. It may be sudden and dramatic, or gradual and cumulative. But in any case it's a new beginning. Following Jesus' words to Nicodemus, "You must be born anew" (John 3:7 RSV), we speak of this conversion as rebirth, new life in Christ, or regeneration.

Following Paul and Luther, John Wesley called this process *justification*. Justification is what happens when Christians abandon all those vain attempts to justify themselves before God, to be seen as "just" in God's eyes through religious and moral practices. It's a time when God's "justifying grace" is experienced and accepted, a time of pardon and forgiveness, of new peace and joy and love. Indeed, we're justified by God's grace through faith.

Justification is also a time of *repentance*—turning away from behaviors rooted in sin and toward actions that express God's love. In this conversion we can expect to receive *assurance* of our present salvation through the Holy Spirit "bearing witness with our spirit that we are children of God" (Romans 8:16).

Growing in grace

Conversion is but the beginning of the new life of wholeness. Through what Wesley called God's "sanctifying grace," we can continue to grow. In fact, Wesley affirmed, we're to press on, with God's help, in the path of *sanctification,* the gift of Christian perfection. The goal of the sanctified life is to be perfected in love, to experience the pure love of God and others, a holiness of heart and life, a total death to sin. We're not there yet; but by God's grace, as we United Methodists say, "we're going on to perfection!"

For Reflection

1. In your journey of faith, what has been the place of "salvation by grace through faith"? What has been your experience of conversion, whether sudden or gradual?
2. What's your belief about continued growth in grace? In what sense are you "going on to perfection"?

United Methodist

35 We Rely on the Bible

We say that the Bible is vital to our faith and life, but what exactly is the Bible? Here are four ways to view it:

A library

The Bible is a collection of sixty-six books, thirty-nine in the Old Testament (or Hebrew Bible) and twenty-seven in the New Testament. These books were written over a one-thousand-year period in three languages: Hebrew, Aramaic (the language Jesus spoke), and Greek.

The books are of different lengths and different literary styles. In the Hebrew Bible we find legends, histories, liturgies for community worship, songs, proverbs, sermons, even a poetic drama (Job). In the New Testament are Gospels, a history, many letters, and an apocalypse (Revelation). Yet through it all the Bible is the story of the one God, who stands in a covenant relationship with the people of God.

Sacred Scripture

In early times and over many generations, the sixty-six books were thoughtfully used by faithful people. In the process their merits were weighed, and the community of believers finally gave them special authority. Tested by faith, proven by experience, these books have become sacred; they've become our rule for faith and practice.

In Israel the Book of Deuteronomy was adopted as the Word of God about 621 B.C. The Torah, or Law (the first five books of the Hebrew Bible), assumed authority around 400 B.C.; the Prophets about 200 B.C.; and the Writings about 100 B.C. After a struggle the Christians determined that the Hebrew Bible was Scripture for them as well. The New Testament as we know it was formed and adopted by church councils between A.D. 200 and A.D. 400.

God's Word

We say that God speaks to us through the Bible, that it's God's Word. This authority derives from three sources:

- We hold that the writers of the Bible were inspired, that they were filled with God's Spirit as they wrote the truth to the best of their knowledge.
- We hold that God was at work in the process of canonization, during which only the most faithful and useful books were adopted as Scripture.

- We hold that the Holy Spirit works today in our thoughtful study of the Scriptures, especially as we study them together, seeking to relate the old words to life's present realities.

The Bible's authority is, therefore, nothing magical. For example, we do not open the text at random to discover God's will. The authority of Scripture derives from the movement of God's Spirit in times past and in our reading of it today.

A guide to faith and life

We United Methodists put the Bible to work. In congregational worship we read from the Bible. Through preaching, we interpret its message for our lives. It forms the background of most of our hymns and liturgy. It's the foundation of our church school curriculum. Many of us use it in our individual devotional lives, praying through its implications day by day. However, we admit that there's still vast "biblical illiteracy" in our denomination. We need to help one another open the Bible and use it.

Perhaps the Bible is best put to use when we seriously answer these four questions about a given text: (1) What did this passage mean to its original hearers? (2) What part does it play in the Bible's total witness? (3) What does God seem to be saying to my life, my community, my world, through this passage? and (4) What changes should I consider making as a result of my study?

For Reflection

1. What parts of the Bible have influenced you most? What differences has the Bible made in your life? Share with others.
2. What has been your pattern of Bible study in recent years? Are there any changes you would like to make?

Member's Handbook

36 We Are Nourished in Holy Communion

Like baptism, Holy Communion is regarded by Protestants as a sacrament. That is, it's an act of worship *ordained by Christ* and is a *means of grace.* This does not mean that we become any more worthy of God's grace by taking part in Communion. Rather, we open ourselves to the divine love that's already there; we become more ready to receive that love and to respond to it.

As with baptism, we use common, physical gifts of the earth, bread and wine—though in United Methodist churches we prefer unfermented grape juice. All Christians are welcome at our table, whatever their denomination. Holy Communion is a family meal, and all Christians are members of Christ's family. Therefore, in each congregation, when we receive the bread and cup, we join with millions of brothers and sisters across the ages and around the world.

Holy Communion (or the Lord's Supper) is a mystery too deep for words. Its meaning will vary for each of us and from one time to another. But three essential meanings are caught up in this proclamation in our Communion service: "Christ has died; Christ is risen; Christ will come again" (*The United Methodist Hymnal*, p. 14).

"Christ has died"

In part, Communion is a time to remember Jesus' death, his self-giving sacrifice on our behalf. As he said to the disciples at their last meal together, "Do this in remembrance of me" (1 Corinthians 11:24).

In remembering his passion and crucifixion, we remember our own guilt; for we know that in our sin we crucify Christ many times over from day to day. So the Lord's Supper is a time of confession: "We confess that we have not loved you with our whole heart....We have not heard the cry of the needy" (*The United Methodist Hymnal*, p. 12).

"Christ is risen"

But Communion is not a memorial service for a dead Jesus. It's not a time to wallow in our own guilt. It's a time to celebrate the Resurrection, to recognize and give thanks for the Risen Christ. The bread and wine represent the living presence of Christ among us—though we do not claim, as some denominations do, that they *become* Christ's body and blood.

In Luke's Resurrection story, the Risen Christ broke bread with two of his followers at Emmaus, "then their eyes were opened, and they recognized him" (24:31). So, as we're nourished by this meal, our eyes are opened; and we recognize Christ here in our congregation, our community, and our world. What's our response? Thanksgiving! In fact, another of our words for Communion, the *Eucharist,* means thanksgiving.

"Christ will come again"

In Communion we also celebrate the final victory of Christ. We anticipate God's coming reign, God's future for this world and all creation. As Jesus said, "I tell you, I will never again drink of this fruit of the vine until that day when I drink it new with you in my Father's kingdom" (Matthew 26:29).

We believe that we're partners with God in creating this future, but the demands of discipleship are rigorous. In the bread and wine of the Lord's Supper, in the fellowship of Christian friends gathered at his table, we find the nourishment we need for the tasks of discipleship ahead. The Risen Christ is with us! We're new creatures! We're ready for ministry in his world!

For Reflection

1. With the help of your pastor or other leader, study "A Service of Word and Table II," *The United Methodist Hymnal,* pages 12-15.
2. Recall and share with others some times when Holy Communion has been especially meaningful to you. How could you grow further in your appreciation of the Lord's Supper?

United Methodist

37 We Follow the Holy Spirit

The Holy Spirit is God's present activity in our midst. When we sense God's leading, God's challenge, or God's support or comfort, we say that it's the Holy Spirit at work.

In Hebrew, the words for *Spirit, wind,* and *breath* are nearly the same. The same is true in Greek. In trying to describe God's activity among them, the ancients were saying that it was like God's breath, like a sacred wind. It could not be seen or held: "The wind blows where it chooses, and you hear the sound of it, but you do not know where it comes from or where it goes" (John 3:8). But the effect of God's Spirit, like the wind, could be felt and known. Where do we find the evidence of the Spirit at work?

In the Bible

The Spirit is mentioned often throughout the Bible. In Genesis a "wind from God swept over the face of the waters," as if taking part in the Creation (1:2). Later in the Old Testament (Hebrew Bible), we often read of "the Spirit of the Lord."

In Matthew's account of Jesus' baptism, Jesus "saw the Spirit of God descending like a dove and alighting on him" (3:16) and he "was led up by the Spirit into the wilderness to be tempted" (4:1). After his Resurrection Christ told his disciples, "You will receive power when the Holy Spirit has come upon you" (Acts 1:8). A few weeks later, on the Day of Pentecost, this came to pass: "And suddenly from heaven there came a sound like the rush of a violent wind.... All of them were filled with the Holy Spirit" (Acts 2:2, 4). As the Book of Acts and Paul's letters attest, from that time on, the early Christians were vividly aware of God's Spirit leading the new church.

In guidance, comfort, and strength

Today we continue to experience God's breath, God's Spirit. As one of our creeds puts it, "We believe in the Holy Spirit, God present with us for guidance, for comfort, and for strength" (*The United Methodist Hymnal,* No. 884). We sense the Spirit in time alone—perhaps in prayer, in our study of the Scriptures, in reflection on a difficult decision, or in the memory of a loved one. The Spirit's touch is intensely personal.

Perhaps we're even more aware of the Holy Spirit in the community of believers—the congregation, the church school class or fellowship group, the soup kitchen, the planning committee, the prayer meeting, the family.

Somehow the Spirit speaks through the thoughtful and loving interaction of God's people. The Holy Spirit, who brought the church into being, is still guiding and upholding it, if we will but listen.

In the gifts we receive

How does the Holy Spirit affect our lives? By changing us! By renewing us and by strengthening us for the work of ministry.

- *Fruits:* Jesus said, "You will know them by their fruits" (Matthew 7:16). What sort of fruit? Paul asserts that "the fruit of the Spirit is love, joy, peace, patience, kindness, generosity, faithfulness, gentleness, and self-control" (Galatians 5:22).
- *Gifts:* Paul also writes that the Spirit bestows spiritual gifts on believers. In 1 Corinthians 12:8-10 he lists nine, which vary from one person to another: the utterance of wisdom, the utterance of knowledge, faith, healing, working of miracles, prophecy, the discernment of spirits, various kinds of tongues, and the interpretation of tongues.

These fruits and gifts are not of our own achievement. They and others are the outgrowth of the Spirit's work in us, by grace, through our faith in Jesus the Christ. And they are not given for personal gain. Through these fruits and gifts, the Holy Spirit empowers us for ministry in the world.

For Reflection

1. In what situations have you sensed God's Spirit at work? Describe.
2. What gifts or fruits would you say the Spirit has brought into your life? For what others do you still yearn?

Member's Handbook

38 We Live as Disciples

A disciple is one who follows a master teacher, who learns from the master, and who attempts to live out the master's teachings. In the first century, Jesus was not alone in having disciples. John the Baptist had such followers, as did other religious teachers. To United Methodists, living as a disciple of Jesus Christ means at least the following:

Doing the gospel

Jesus chose his closest disciples. "Follow me," he said, and they followed. But they soon discovered that his teaching was not simply a new idea, but a new way of being and doing in the world. Discipleship, they learned, is the active side of faith. It's *doing* the gospel and *doing* faith. "Not everyone who says to me, 'Lord, Lord,' will enter the kingdom of heaven, but only the one who does the will of my Father in heaven" (Matthew 7:21).

Since the earliest days of the Wesleyan revival in England, the Methodists have been known as "doers of the word, and not merely hearers" (James 1:22).

Faith and works

The Protestant Reformers saw the tendency to claim salvation as the reward of "good works" as one of the problems in the sixteenth-century Roman church. Even monetary gifts to the church were seen as works by which one might escape some years in purgatory. Luther and others rejected such "works righteousness," proclaiming that we are saved by grace through faith alone.

But two centuries later Wesley believed that the reformers had gone too far, that they had not given good works the proper emphasis. He kept faith and works in balance; we're saved through faith, but true faith inevitably shows itself in moral action, in ministry. "Faith without works is...dead" (James 2:26).

Personal and social discipleship

Our discipleship, or ministry, is to be acted out in all sorts of circumstances. In topic 6, "We Minister," we recognized four general avenues for ministry: (1) in our daily activity, (2) through new initiatives, (3) through groups and institutions, and (4) through the church.

In all these we need to keep a balance between personal and social discipleship. Some may address the needs of individuals on a face-to-face basis but neglect the larger societal issues where Christian action is needed. Others may plunge headlong into social causes, while overlooking the hurts of the people around them. Both are necessary.

Requirements for discipleship

What does it take to be a disciple of Christ?

- *Faith:* Discipleship must be rooted in our faithful response to God's grace in Jesus Christ. Without faith, our ministry is just so much frantic effort.
- *Prayer:* We cannot find our way in discipleship all alone. We need to be open to the direction and power of the Holy Spirit, and this requires prayer.
- *Preparation:* Some discipleship comes naturally for people of faith. But some requires study or thought or training or planning. It requires equipping "the saints for the work of ministry" (Ephesians 4:12).
- *Discipline:* United Methodists have long recognized that it takes a firm commitment to follow Christ in the world. There will be temptations, obstacles, and defeats. We will need consistent personal discipline if we're to follow through to the end.
- *Accountability:* We will not be able to stay the course alone. We need Christian friends who will help hold us accountable as the sort of disciples we're determined to be.

For Reflection

1. In the past week or so, what have been some expressions of your discipleship?
2. Describe situations in your community where both personal and social discipleship is needed. What responses could you make?

United Methodist

39 We Act in Society

From the beginning, the various branches of the Methodist family of churches have had a concern for social justice. In recent decades, at each General Conference session, United Methodists have updated a lengthy document called the "Social Principles." Part of our *Book of Discipline,* this statement serves as a guide to official church action and our individual witness. Here is an overview of the six sections of the "Social Principles:"

The natural world

We affirm that we're responsible for the way we use the Lord's creation. We support social policies that promote the wise use of water, air, soil, minerals, and plants. We support the conservation of energy and oppose energy-using technologies that threaten human health. We're concerned for the humane treatment of animals and the respectful use of space.

The nurturing community

We affirm the family and work to strengthen its relationships. We affirm the sanctity of marriage and shared fidelity between a man and a woman. We recognize divorce as regrettable and intend to minister to the members of divorced families. We affirm the integrity of single persons. We recognize that sexuality is a good gift of God and that sex between a man and woman is only to be clearly affirmed in the marriage bond. We recognize the tragic conflicts of life with life that may justify abortion and urge prayerful consideration by all parties involved. We assert the right of every person to die with dignity.

The social community

We affirm all persons as equally valuable in God's sight. We reject racism and assert the rights of racial minorities to equal opportunities in employment, education, voting, housing, and leadership. We urge social practices that will uphold the rights of religious minorities, of children, youth, young adults, and the aging, of women, and of disabled persons. We affirm our long-standing support of abstinence from alcohol and illegal drugs, and we support the rehabilitation of drug-dependent persons.

The economic community

All economic systems are under the judgment of God. We believe the private ownership of property is a trusteeship under God and must be responsibly managed. We support the right of employees and employers to organize for collective bargaining. We affirm the right of safe and meaningful work and creative leisure. We support efforts to ensure truth in pricing, packaging, lending, and advertising; and we urge people to evaluate their consumption of goods in the light of the quality of life. We call on Christians to abstain from gambling and to be in ministry with persons who are the victims of this societal menace.

The political community

We hold governments responsible for the protection of people's basic freedoms. We believe that neither church nor state should attempt to dominate the other. We call for freedom of information and quality education. We defend the right of individuals to practice conscientious, non-violent civil disobedience. We support government measures to reduce crimes consistent with the basic freedoms of persons; and we urge the creation of new systems of rehabilitation.

The world community

God's world is one world. We hold nations accountable for unjust treatment of their citizens. We affirm the right of people in developing nations to shape their own destiny; and we applaud efforts to establish a more just international economic order. We believe war is incompatible with the teachings of Christ, and we claim that it is the primary moral duty of every nation to resolve disputes peacefully. We endorse the United Nations and commend all who pursue world peace through law.

For Reflection

1. You may wish to study the "Social Principles" in full. The full text is found in *The Book of Discipline of The United Methodist Church—2004*, pages 95-125.
2. Think about ways in which you could employ the "Social Principles" in your community and your world.

Member's Handbook

40 We Expect God's Reign

In topic 26 we said that Christian faith is, in part, a matter of hoping. We believe in and trust the Lord of the future, and we lean into the future that God has promised. God goes before us, beckoning us into the new world that is already being created, calling us to join in the challenging work of fashioning it.

However, when we're confronted with personal disasters or with the daily horror stories of society's ills, we may falter. Hope may seem to be unrealistic, naive optimism.

Yet our hope is not in trends. Our hope is in the Lord of all creation and all history—a God who is still in charge and is actively at work transforming the world. How do we know this?

The coming *shalom*

The Bible is a book of God's promises. It may seem to be about the past, but its outlook is toward the future. From promises in the Book of Genesis to Abraham and Sarah for a new land, a son, and countless descendants (chapter 17), to promises in the Book of Revelation of a "new heaven and a new earth" (21:1), God was helping biblical people live into the vision of creation's ultimate goal.

The Old Testament (Hebrew Bible) uses the word *shalom* to describe God's future. We often translate this word as "peace," but it means more than that. *Shalom* means a world of plenty, of personal and interpersonal harmony and righteousness, of liberation, of just economic practices, and of ordered political relations.

The coming kingdom

For Jesus, the *shalom* of God was the kingdom of God, the coming reign of God in human hearts and in all human affairs. In fact he proclaimed that this reign already "has come near" (Mark 1:15) and that the decision about one's part in it was an urgent necessity: "Strive first for the kingdom of God and his righteousness" (Matthew 6:33).

In the resurrection of our Lord, his amazed followers recognized that God's reign was breaking into their lives: "So if anyone is in Christ, there is a new creation: everything old has passed away; see, everything has become new!" (2 Corinthians 5:17). The old regime of hostility, greed, injustice, and violence was obsolete and dying. The new order was coming in: "See, I am making all things new" (Revelation 21:5). For those who see with the eyes of faith, it is apparent that our common human future on earth is indeed the promised reign of God.

The church as a sign of the future

There are signs of the coming Kingdom all about us—from random acts of kindness by individuals to the worldwide family's growth in tolerance and cooperation. In particular we see the church as a sign of the Kingdom. Imperfect as it is, the community of believers nevertheless provides the best clue we have to God's vision. Day after day, we see deeds of Christian courage, of compassion and reconciliation, of integrity in the face of temptation, and of witness for truth and justice.

Our part

And what is our role—to sit back and simply wait for God's kingdom to arrive? By no means! We are to pray earnestly for the Kingdom to come on earth (Matthew 6:10). We are to watch faithfully for any signs of its coming (Matthew 25:13). We are to put away our old selves and clothe ourselves "with the new self, created according to the likeness of God in true righteousness and holiness" (Ephesians 4:24). As renewed people, we're to do "the work of ministry" (Ephesians 4:12). As Easter people witness and serve, we take part in the Kingdom's dawning. Thy Kingdom come!

For Reflection

1. It's often difficult to believe that the future is in God's hands. List and consider signs of the dawning Kingdom that you have observed in the church and the world.
2. Think of ways that you can become a catalyst for change in your family, church, community, and the world.

United Methodist

Our Congregation at a Glance

For use with topics 1 and 2

1. The name of our local church is _____

   Address: _____

   Phone: _____

2. We are a congregation of _____ (No.) members. Over the last five years our membership has been growing ( ), declining ( ), or holding steady ( ). Otherwise, our congregation seems to be changing in these ways:

   _____

3. Our congregation's make-up by age is _____

   Our make-up by race and ethnic group is _____

4. Most of our members reside in _____

   Most work in _____

   In general, our church serves the _____ community.

5. The mission of our congregation: _____

   _____

6. We have ___ (No.) church school classes for children, ___ for youth, ___ for adults. We have these other educational groups or activities:

   _____

7. We support these opportunities for service and witness: _____

   _____

8. In addition, there are these other major activities and small-group activities: _____

9. Some of our congregation's major strengths are _____

   _____

10. Some of the ways our congregation needs to grow are _____

    _____

Our United Methodist Organization

For use with topics 8 and 9

1. Our jurisdiction: _____

2. Our episcopal area: _____ Our bishop: _____
   Office at: _____

3. Our annual conference: _____
   Office at: _____

4. Our district: _____ District superintendent: _____
   Office at: _____

5. Other congregations with which ours is grouped: _____

6. Our congregation's administrative body: _____
   Chairperson: _____ Meeting times: _____

7. Our congregation's programming body (if different): _____
   Chairperson: _____ Meeting times: _____

8. Administrative committees: _____

9. Ministry areas and groups: _____

10. Lay leader(s): _____

11. Lay member(s) of annual conference: _____

12. Our pastor: _____ Office phone: _____

13. Other church staff: _____

For Further Study

- *A Brief History of The United Methodist Church.* Nashville: Discipleship Resources, 1998.
- *Affirmations of The United Methodist Church: Beliefs and Convictions of The United Methodist Church From the 1996 Book of Discipline.* Nashville: Discipleship Resources, 1998.
- Behney, J. Bruce and Eller, Paul H. *The History of The Evangelical United Brethren Church.* Nashville: Abingdon Press, 1979.
- Benedict, Daniel T., Jr. *Come to the Waters: Baptism and Our Ministry of Welcoming Seekers and Making Disciples.* Nashville: Discipleship Resources, 1997.
- Carder, Kenneth L. *Living Our Beliefs: The United Methodist Way.* Nashville: Discipleship Resources, 1996.
- Custer, Chester E. *The United Methodist Primer: 2005 Revised Edition.* Nashville: Discipleship Resources, 1986.
- Felton, Gayle Carlton. *By Water and the Spirit: Making Connections for Identity and Ministry.* Nashville: Discipleship Resources, 1997.
- _____. *This Holy Mystery: A United Methodist Understanding of Holy Communion.* Nashville: Discipleship Resources, 2005
- *Foundations: Shaping the Ministry of Christian Education in Your Congregation.* Nashville: Discipleship Resources, 1993.
- Hickman, Hoyt L. *Worshiping With United Methodists: A Guide for Pastors and Church Leaders.* Nashville: Abingdon Press, 1996.
- Logan, James C. *How Great a Flame! Contemporary Lessons from the Wesleyan Revival.* Nashville: Discipleship Resources, 2005.
- Mansker, Steve, et. al. *A Perfect Love Understanding John Wesley's "A Plain Account of Christian Perfection."* Nashville: Discipleship Resources, 2004.
- McAnally, Thomas S. *Questions and Answers About The United Methodist Church.* Nashville: Abingdon Press, 1995.
- Stamm, Mark W. *Sacraments and Discipleship: Understanding Baptism and the Lord's Supper in a United Methodist Context.* Nashville: Discipleship Resources, 2000.
- Thurston, Branson L. *The United Methodist Way.* Nashville: Discipleship Resources, 1997.

In addition, the devotional guides *Alive Now, The Upper Room, Pockets, Devo'Zine,* and *Weavings* may be ordered from The Upper Room (www.upperroom.org or 800-925-6847).

For the Group Leader

If you're planning to have a group study using *The United Methodist Member's Handbook,* this section is for you. The handbook is a membership orientation resource organized around three major themes in the meaning of church membership: (1) *belonging* to the congregation and the larger church; (2) *remembering* our Judaic-Christian and denominational story; and (3) *believing* in the gospel of Jesus the Christ.

Participants and settings. The handbook stands on its own as a helpful study book for individuals, senior-high-school age through adult. But learning will be greatly enhanced by using it in a group, where participants and leaders can share their questions and answers, their Christian experience, and their faith. It's designed for use by groups such as these:

- *Inquirers:* People wanting to know more about the church as background for their decision regarding membership;
- *Prospective members:* Constituents and others who intend to become members when the course is completed;
- *Transfers:* People coming from other churches, United Methodist or not;
- *Those professing faith:* New Christians, with or without background in the church;
- *Current members:* People with some years in the church but who want a refresher course.

Though the handbook provides a useful overview for confirmation preparation, it's not recommended as a substitute for official United Methodist confirmation resources for youth; and it is beyond the reading level of most eleven- to fourteen-year-olds in such groups.

You might consider such settings as these: Sunday morning membership class, adult church school class, Sunday evening or midweek series, summer or Lenten series, weekend retreat, storefront or retirement home ministry, new congregation or interchurch ministry. The possibilities are endless. What is the need where you are?

Leadership. The pastor or other church staff member may be in the best position to lead this study, but this not essential. For some subjects, such as those involving how we live out our faith in the world, lay leaders can bring exceptional insight. Perhaps best of all would be a clergy-lay leadership team in which one or another leader would take responsibility for each topic, based on background and strengths.

Because of the broad scope of this study, the material is not easily "covered" through class presentations. Each topic is a rich subject in its own right and could easily consume an entire session—and few participants would want to commit to forty sessions!

Therefore, class members' outside study of each topic in advance is highly recommended. The leader should make a clear assignment of a manageable number of topics for each session. These assignments could include: (a) reading and underlining the text; (b) noting questions to raise in class discussion; (c) studying related resources; (d) preparing brief class reports; and/or (e) writing out answers to the questions and suggestions in the "For Reflection" section at the end of each topic. In this way class time can be used for exploration and interaction among the participants, a more effective learning style than the presentation of facts.

You can't do everything in a short course. The important thing is to lay a vital foundation for continuing growth. This will happen through the quality of personal relationships you foster, the basic mental tools and spirit of open inquiry you share, and your own earnest commitment to the church and the journey of faith.

Schedule. One of the most workable patterns for scheduling this study is on a weekly basis. Allow for at least one hour per session; an hour and a half is preferable.

The study is organized not by sessions, but in forty topics, each standing fairly independently. The order in which these are treated can easily be altered. Indeed, the sequence of the three major parts can be changed. You may, for example, wish to start with Part Two, "We Remember."

You will probably want to group several topics together for study in a single session. Here's a suggested grouping for twelve sessions: 1-2, 3-7, 8-11, 12-15, 16-18, 19-21, 22-25, 26-28, 29-30, 31-33, 34-36, 37-40. For six sessions you could give two periods to each of the three major parts.

It's a privilege to lead others in the study of such fundamental issues—the meaning of membership in Christ's church, the story of faithful people through the ages, our lifelong journeys of faith and discipleship, our essential beliefs, and more. May the Holy Spirit be your guide!